The Character of Jesus

Publishers: FIELDREAMS INC.

ISBN: 978-1-7774536-1-9

Email: gordiannweke2@gmail.com

Phone: +234 8095178210

Contents

"Let this mind be in you, which was also in Christ Jesus: [6] Who, being in the form of God, thought it not robbery to be equal with God: [7] But made himself of no reputation, and took upon him the form of a servant, and was made in the likeness of men: [8] And being found in fashion as a man, he humbled himself, and became obedient unto death, even the death of the cross. [9] Wherefore God also hath highly exalted him, and given him a name which is above every name: [10] That at the name of Jesus every knee should bow, of things in heaven, and things in earth, and things under the earth; [11] And that every tongue should confess that Jesus Christ is Lord, to the glory of God the Father" *Philippians 2:5-11.*

APPRECIATION

My deepest appreciation goes to my Lord Jesus for choosing to reveal himself through his Spirit to the church in this season. I wish to express my special thanks to my wife Chinelo, and my sons David, Joseph and Emmanuel for their continued support. I am grateful to my brother Ogochukwu Nweke for taking time to review this material. My sincere appreciation also goes to my siblings, Chinyelu and Anthony for their consistent prayers and support. Finally, my earnest thanksgiving and praise goes to the Father from whom all good things come.

DEDICATION

This book is dedicated to my mother, Mercy, for bringing me up in the fear of the Lord and for steadfastly interceding for me.

A sequel to the '**Revelation of Jesus**', The Character of Jesus focuses on the humanity of Jesus. While on earth, the Lord Jesus was one hundred percent God and one hundred percent man. He lived and walked like any other person in his environment but without sin. In this book, the Lord desires to show his exemplary character as a landmark for his children. He unveils his human nature and attributes that distinguish him from all other persons. By his conduct, the Lord seeks to teach his people that it is possible to live a responsible and blameless life on earth. By the anointing of the Holy Spirit which he received and has made available to every believer, the Lord instructs that his children have been properly equipped to deal with the issues and challenges of life.

A careful study of this material would provide the

essential ingredients and information required to live a godly life on earth. Observing, practising and sharing these principles as outlined by the Lord would ensure a victorious and most successful life for the people of God.

We have quoted the scriptures extensively from the New King James version of the bible except where indicated otherwise. May you be strengthened with might by the Holy Spirit to practice the precepts in this material as you read and yield yourself to his instructions. God bless you.

1

LOVE

In the gospel of John, the Lord said, ***"Greater love hath no man than this that a man lay down his life for his friends"*** *John 15:13.*

Jesus is the embodiment of love. Every decision, word and action he took while on Earth was founded on love. He showed love to all around him even at the point of death. God expects his children to show this measure of love to all around them. As children of God, we are the products and offspring of love. When we received Christ, we were given his new nature, the nature of love, that nature begins to function and dominate our thoughts, words and action, as we fellowship with the Holy Spirit in prayer and study of the word. When a child is born, he is one hundred percent human. As he is fed, his body and faculties begin to develop and grow. Unless he is taught, he may never know how to talk, walk, respond or behave appropriately. That is why as God's child, you are required to be taught with God's word. You are required to subject yourself under the authority of God's word and God's Spirit. It is essential to be a member of the family of God in a living church. Every born again child of God has been given God's nature of love. Most are unaware of that nature and are unable to function in it. In the book of Romans, the bible says, ***"And hope maketh not ashamed; because the love of God is shed abroad in our hearts by the Holy Ghost which is given unto us".*** *Romans 5:5.*

The Holy Spirit who we received from God has filled our hearts with God's love. Thus we can effectively function in God's love. First we must be aware that we have received God's nature of love. Secondly we must study God's word to learn how to function in that love. Oftentimes, it may be difficult to understand scripture without being instructed. That is why it is very necessary to belong to a living local church. As a member of a church, you are under the guidance of a pastor and other church leaders. Under their guidance, you will be taught and given necessary support to grow effectively as a believer. The church serves to provide the nourishment and support required for your growth and development. The pastor would provide the answers you require when faced with questions and challenges as you progress in your

Christian growth. In the gospel of John, Jesus said, ***"For God so loved the world that he gave his only begotten Son, that whosoever believeth in him should not perish, but have everlasting life. [17] For God sent not his Son into the world to condemn the world; but that the world through him might be saved"*** *John 3:16-17.*

From above scripture, we learn that Jesus was the product of God's love. Secondly, the active ingredient of love is giving. The ability to willingly give without reservation is the hallmark of love. God showed this love when he sent his Son Jesus to the world. Jesus manifested this quality of love when he offered himself to God for the remission of man's sins. The God kind of love requires us to be selfless in our dealings with others. In one of his teachings, Jesus provided a better path than the provisions of the Mosaic Law,

"Ye have heard that it hath been said, An eye for an eye, and a tooth for a tooth: [39] But I say unto you, That ye resist not evil: but whosoever shall smite thee on thy right cheek, turn to him the other also. [40] And if any man will sue thee at the law, and take away thy coat, let him have thy cloke also. [41] And whosoever shall compel thee to go a mile, go with him twain. [42] Give to him that asketh thee, and from him that would borrow of thee turn not thou away. [43] Ye have heard that it hath been said, Thou shalt love thy neighbour, and hate thine enemy. [44] But I say unto you, Love your enemies, bless them that curse you, do good to them that hate you, and pray for them which despitefully use you, and persecute you; [45] That ye may be the children of your Father which is in heaven: for he maketh his sun to rise on the evil and on the

good, and sendeth rain on the just and on the unjust" *Matthew 5:38-45*

Jesus clearly explained how children of God are expected to conduct themselves in a wicked world. Apostle Paul in his letter to the church at Ephesus admonished, ***"Be ye therefore followers of God, as dear children; [2] And walk in love, as Christ also hath loved us, and hath given himself for us an offering and a sacrifice to God for a sweet smelling savour"***
Ephesians 5:1-2.

Apostle John in his epistle to the churches emphasized this point when he said, ***"Beloved, let us love one another: for love is of God; and every one that loveth is born of God, and knoweth God. [8] He that loveth not knoweth not God; for God is love. [9] In this was manifested the love of God toward us, because***

that God sent his only begotten Son into the world, that we might live through him. [10] Herein is love, not that we loved God, but that he loved us, and sent his Son to be the propitiation for our sins. [11] Beloved, if God so loved us, we ought also to love one another" *1 John 4:7-11.*

In his letter to the church in Rome, Paul said, ***"Owe no man anything, but to love one another: for he that loveth another hath fulfilled the law. [9] For this, Thou shalt not commit adultery, Thou shalt not kill, Thou shalt not steal, Thou shalt not bear false witness, Thou shalt not covet; and if there be any other commandment, it is briefly comprehended in this saying, namely, Thou shalt love thy neighbour as thyself. [10] Love worketh no ill to his neighbour: therefore love is the fulfilling of the law"*** *Romans 13:8-10.*

Apostle John compared loving others to walking in the light when he said, ***"He that saith he is in the light, and hateth his brother, is in darkness even until now. [10] He that loveth his brother abideth in the light, and there is none occasion of stumbling in him. [11] But he that hateth his brother is in darkness, and walketh in darkness, and knoweth not whither he goeth, because that darkness hath blinded his eyes"*** *1 John 2:9-11.*

Apostle John expressly distinguishes the children of God from the children of the devil thus, ***"In this the children of God are manifest, and the children of the devil: whosoever doeth not righteousness is not of God, neither he that loveth not his brother"*** *1 John 3:10.*

Apostle Paul listed love as the first fruit of the recreated human spirit, ***"But if ye be led of the***

Spirit, ye are not under the law. [19] Now the works of the flesh are manifest, which are these; Adultery, fornication, uncleanness, lasciviousness, [20] Idolatry, witchcraft, hatred, variance, emulations, wrath, strife, seditions, heresies, [21] Envying, murders, drunkenness, reveling, and such like: of the which I tell you before, as I have also told you in time past, that they which do such things shall not inherit the kingdom of God. [22] But the fruit of the Spirit is love, joy, peace, longsuffering, gentleness, goodness, faith, [23] Meekness, temperance: against such there is no law"

Galatians 5:18-23.

Apostle Paul gave an awesome lesson on love as follows, ***"If I speak in the tongues of men and of angels, but have not love, I am only a resounding gong or a clanging cymbal. If I have***

the gift of prophecy and can fathom all mysteries and all knowledge, and if I have a faith that can move mountains, but have not love, I am nothing. If I give all I possess to the poor and surrender my body to the flames, but have not love, I gain nothing. Love is patient, love is kind. It does not envy, it does not boast, it is not proud. It is not rude, it is not self-seeking, it is not easily angered, it keeps no record of wrong. Love does not delight in evil but rejoices with the truth. It always protects, always trusts, always hopes, always perseveres. Love never fails. But where there are prophecies, they will cease; where there are tongues, they will be stilled; where there is knowledge, it will pass away. For we know in part and we prophecy in part, but when perfection comes, the imperfect disappears". *1 Corinthians 13:1-10 [NIV]*

Apostle Paul concluded his lesson by saying, ***"And now these three remain: faith, hope and love. But the greatest of these is love".*** *1 Corinthians 13:13 [NIV]*

12

2

HUMILITY

In his letter to the Philippians church, Apostle Paul gave a vivid description of the life of Jesus when he wrote, ***"Let this mind be in you, which was also in Christ Jesus: [6] Who, being in the form of God, thought it not robbery to be equal with God: [7] But made himself of no reputation, and took upon him the form of a servant, and was made in the likeness of men: [8] And being found in fashion as a man, he humbled himself, and became obedient unto death, even the death of the cross. [9] Wherefore God also hath highly exalted him, and given him a name which is above every name: [10] That at the name of***

Jesus every knee should bow, of things in heaven, and things in earth, and things under the earth; [11] And that every tongue should confess that Jesus Christ is Lord, to the glory of God the Father" *Philippians 2:5-11.*

Jesus humbled himself to the will of the Father. The prophet Isaiah talked about him before his birth when he wrote, ***"All we like sheep have gone astray; we have turned everyone to his own way; and the Lord hath laid on him the iniquity of us all. [7] He was oppressed, and he was afflicted, yet he opened not his mouth: he is brought as a lamb to the slaughter, and as a sheep before her shearers is dumb, so he openeth not his mouth. [8] He was taken from prison and from judgment: and who shall declare his generation? For he was cut off out of the land of the living: for the transgression of***

my people was he stricken" *Isaiah 53:6-8.*

Jesus emphasized this essential attribute when he taught his disciples while on Earth, he said, ***"Come unto me, all ye that labour and are heavy laden and I will give you rest. [29] Take my yoke upon you, and learn of me; for I am meek and lowly in heart: and ye shall find rest unto your souls"*** *Matthew 11:28-29.*

The Lord in the above statement encouraged us to learn from him the quality of gentleness and humility. These he said will produce peace and rest for our souls. At the last supper with his disciples, the Lord Jesus took a bowl of water and washed the feet of his disciples, after which he said, ***"Ye call me Master and Lord: and ye say well; for so I am. [14] If I then, your Lord and Master, have washed your feet; ye also ought to wash one another's feet. [15]***

For I have given you an example, that ye should do as I have done to you". *John 13:13-15.*

Apostle Peter in his epistle to the churches admonished, ***"Likewise, ye younger, submit yourselves unto the elder. Yea, all of you be subject one to another, and be clothed with humility: for God resisteth the proud, and giveth grace to the humble. [6] Humble yourselves therefore under the mighty hand of God, that he may exalt you in due time"*** *1 Peter 5:5-6.*

The Lord Jesus told a beautiful story to illustrate the effect of humility. ***"Two men went up into the temple to pray; the one a Pharisee, and the other a publican. [11] The Pharisee stood and prayed thus with himself, God, I thank thee, that I am not as other men are, extortionists, unjust, adulterers, or even as this publican. [12] I fast twice in the week; I give***

tithes of all that I possess. [13] And the publican, standing afar off, would not lift up so much as his eyes unto heaven, but smote upon his breast, saying, God be merciful to me a sinner. [14] I tell you, this man went down to his house justified rather than the other: for every one that exalteth himself shall be abased; and he that humbleth himself shall be exalted" *Luke 18:10-14.*

In the gospel of Luke, Jesus gave a very important teaching to clarify the issue of humility. ***"When thou art bidden of any man to a wedding, sit not down in the highest room; lest a more honorable man than thou be bidden of him; [9] And he that bade thee and him come and say to thee, Give this man place; and thou begin with shame to take the lowest room. [10] But when thou art bidden, go and sit down in the lowest room; that when he that bade thee***

cometh, he may say unto thee, Friend, go up higher: then shalt thou have worship in the presence of them that sit at meat with thee. [11] For whosoever exalteth himself shall be abased; and he that humbleth himself shall be exalted" *Luke 14:8-11.*

In the book of Proverbs, the bible declares that ***"A man's pride shall bring him low: but honour shall uphold the humble in spirit"*** *Proverbs 29:23.*

The Lord expects his children to walk in humility before him and in their dealings with others.

3

RIGHTEOUS

In the book of Hebrews, the bible made reference to the words written by the Psalmist concerning the Christ. The bible says, ***"And again, when he bringeth in the first begotten into the world, he saith, And let all the angels of God worship him. [7] And of the angels he saith, Who maketh his angels spirits, and his ministers a flame of fire. [8] But unto the Son he saith , Thy throne, O God, is for ever and ever: a sceptre of righteousness is the sceptre of thy kingdom. [9] Thou hast loved righteousness, and hated iniquity; therefore God, even thy God, hath anointed thee with the oil of gladness above thy fellows"*** *Hebrews 1:6-9.*

From the scripture above, it is evident that righteousness is an essential requirement for God's upliftment. As born again Christians, we have received a new nature of righteousness from God. Apostle Paul explained this revelation in his letter to the church in Rome, ***"For if by one man's offence death reigned by one; much more they which receive abundance of grace and of the gift of righteousness shall reign in life by one, Jesus Christ.) [18] Therefore as by the offence of one judgment came upon all men to condemnation; even so by the righteousness of one the free gift came upon all men unto justification of life. [19] For as by one man's disobedience many were made sinners, so by the obedience of one shall many be made righteous"*** *Romans 5:17-19.*

When God looks at us, he sees his righteousness, ***"For he hath made him to be sin***

for us, who knew no sin; that we might be made the righteousness of God in him"
2 Corinthians 5:21.

Jesus the righteous one was made sin, and in his place, we were made the righteousness of God. When he hung on the cross, he was made sin. And on him was laid all the righteous requirements of the law. This was why God turned his face away from him, forcing him to cry, ***"And at the ninth hour Jesus cried with a loud voice, saying, Eloi, Eloi, lama sabachthani? Which is, being interpreted, My God, my God, why hast thou forsaken me?"*** *Mark 15:34.*

Having received the nature of righteousness, the lord expects us to develop the character of righteousness. Emphasizing this point, Apostle Paul wrote in his letter to the church in Rome, ***"Let not sin therefore reign in***

your mortal body, that ye should obey it in the lusts thereof. [13] Neither yield ye your members as instruments of unrighteousness unto sin: but yield yourselves unto God, as those that are alive from the dead, and your members as instruments of righteousness unto God". *Romans 6:12-13.*

In the light of the scripture above we can see clearly that it is possible to live unrighteous lives even after receiving the new nature of righteousness. The believer has to choose who to yield himself to. Apostle Paul went further to say, ***"Know ye not, that to whom ye yield yourselves servants to obey, his servants ye are to whom ye obey; whether of sin unto death, or of obedience unto righteousness?"*** *Romans 6:16.*

The child of God must make a conscious effort to live righteously in a sinful world. God's children have been given the ability to live above sin, ***"For sin shall not have dominion over you: for ye are not under the law, but under grace"*** *Romans 6:14.*

Believing and confessing our righteousness is great, but it is not enough. The Lord expects us to live and work our righteousness. Righteous living is a product of our righteous nature. We cannot profess or confess our righteousness while we live in sin. The Psalmist said, ***"Lord, who shall abide in thy tabernacle? Who shall dwell in thy holy hill? [2] He that walketh uprightly, and worketh righteousness, and speaketh the truth in his heart"*** *Psalm 15:1-2.*

The work of righteousness is a duty to which all children of God are called. In the book of Acts, when Peter visited Cornelius, a Gentile,

Peter said, ***"Then Peter opened his mouth, and said, of a truth I perceive that God is no respecter of persons: [35] But in every nation he that feareth him, and worketh righteousness, is accepted with him"*** *Acts 10:34-35.*

Admonishing Christians on proper manner of life, Apostle Paul wrote, ***"Be not deceived: evil communications corrupt good manners. [34] Awake to righteousness, and sin not; for some have not the knowledge of God: I speak this to your shame"***

1 Corinthians 15:33-34.

Paul instructs that believers must be conscious of their righteousness and live accordingly. He went further to emphasize this point when he said, ***"Be ye not unequally yoked together with unbelievers: for what fellowship hath righteousness with unrighteousness? And***

what communion hath light with darkness? [15] And what concord hath Christ with Belial? Or what part hath he that believeth with an infidel? [16] And what agreement hath the temple of God with idols? For ye are the temple of the living God; as God hath said, I will dwell in them, and walk in them; and I will be their God, and they shall be my people. [17] Wherefore come out from among them, and be ye separate, saith the Lord, and touch not the unclean thing; and I will receive you, [18] And will be a Father unto you, and ye shall be my sons and daughters, saith the Lord Almighty. *2 Corinthians 6:14-18.*

Apostle Paul addressed the same issue of righteous living with the Gentile Christians in the church at Ephesus. He wrote, ***"This I say therefore, and testify in the Lord, that ye***

henceforth walk not as other Gentiles walk, in the vanity of their mind, [18] Having the understanding darkened, being alienated from the life of God through the ignorance that is in them, because of the blindness of their heart: [19] Who being past feeling have given themselves over unto lasciviousness, to work all uncleanness with greediness. [20] But ye have not so learned Christ; [21] If so be that ye have heard him, and have been taught by him, as the truth is in Jesus: [22] That ye put off concerning the former conversation the old man, which is corrupt according to the deceitful lusts; [23] And be renewed in the spirit of your mind; [24] And that ye put on the new man, which after God is created in righteousness and true holiness" *Ephesians 4:17-24.*

In his prayer for the Philippians church, Apostle Paul made mention of the fruit of righteousness, ***"And this I pray, that your love may abound yet more and more in knowledge and in all judgment; [10] That ye may approve things that are excellent; that ye may be sincere and without offence till the day of Christ; [11] Being filled with the fruits of righteousness, which are by Jesus Christ, unto the glory and praise of God"*** *Philippians 1:9-11.*

In the book of Proverbs, the bible says, ***"The fruit of the righteous is a tree of life; and he that winneth souls is wise"*** *Proverbs 11:30.*

Recall that the tree of life is one of the trees in the Garden of Eden, which once eaten, produces eternal life. Adam and Eve were prevented from that tree when they sinned against God, lest they eat from it and live forever. The book of Hebrews says, ***"Now no chastening for the present seemeth to be joyous, but grievous: nevertheless afterward it yieldeth the peaceable fruit of righteousness unto them which are exercised thereby"*** *Hebrews 12:11.*

Talking about his transition and his expected reward, Apostle Paul wrote, ***"For I am now ready to be offered, and the time of my departure is at hand. [7] I have fought a good fight, I have finished my course, I have kept the faith: [8] Henceforth there is laid up for me a crown of righteousness, which the Lord, the righteous judge, shall give me at that day: and not to me only, but unto all them also that love his appearing"*** *2 Timothy 4:6-8.*

Prophet Isaiah clearly described the product and consequence of righteousness when he wrote, ***"Until the spirit be poured upon us***

from on high, and the wilderness be a fruitful field, and the fruitful field be counted for a forest. [16] Then judgment shall dwell in the wilderness, and righteousness remain in the fruitful field. [17] And the work of righteousness shall be peace; and the effect of righteousness quietness and assurance for ever"

Isaiah 32:15-17.

4

PRAYERFUL

All through his life and ministry on Earth, the Lord Jesus lived a life of prayer. Prayer here refers to the act or activity of speaking to God in order to give thanks or ask for anything from him. In prayers we address God with thanksgiving, supplication, adoration or confession. At the beginning of his ministry, Jesus went to be baptized and prayed fervently during the occasion. As he prayed, the Holy Ghost came upon him, ***"Now when all the people were baptized, it came to pass, that Jesus also being baptized, and praying, the heaven was opened, [22] And the Holy Ghost descended in a***

***bodily shape like a dove upon him, and a voice came from heaven, which said, Thou art my beloved Son; in thee I am* well pleased"**

Luke 3:21-22.

Jesus was a man of prayer. While on Earth, the bible recorded that he usually went out to solitary places to pray alone. In the gospel of Luke, the bible said, ***"And it came to pass in those days, that he went out into a mountain to pray, and continued all night in prayer to God. [13] And when it was day, he called unto him his disciples: and of them he chose twelve, whom also he named apostles"*** *Luke 6:12-13.*

Its instructive to note from the scripture above that Jesus took out time to pray alone. He continued in prayer all through the night. He prayed fervently before making the major decision of choosing his Apostles. Most of us find it very difficult to pray. When we pray, we do not spend enough time with God. We usually make our decisions and then pray to God for help to achieve our plans. God desires a relationship with his children. Prayer provides the platform for effective communication with God. Healthy relationship is sustained by effective communication. In prayer we talk to God, and listen to hear from him. Prayer opens our eyes to see the hidden mysteries and secrets in God's word. When the eyes of our spirits are opened, we are able to clearly see ourselves the way God sees us. We are also able to understand the mind of God concerning the circumstances we come across and the situations we find ourselves in. When we pray, we talk to God, our spiritual antenna is activated to receive and hear from God. As we fellowship with God's Spirit in prayer, we are lifted and made to participate in divine verities. In the place of prayer we are transported from the physical to the spiritual (supernatural). This is where instructions and decisions are made and carried out. A unique example was given in the book of Luke concerning Jesus, ***"And it came to pass about an eight days after these sayings, he took Peter and John and James, and went up into a mountain to pray. [29] And as he prayed, the fashion of his countenance was altered, and his raiment was white and glistering. [30] And, behold, there talked with him two men, which were Moses and Elias: [31] Who appeared in glory, and spake of his decease which he should accomplish at Jerusalem".*** *Luke 9:28-31.*

The above account talked about the transfiguration or transportation of Jesus from the physical to the spiritual or supernatural. This experience is available to the children of God when they pray. When we pray, especially in the spirit, we are translated to the supernatural and in that realm we can make changes or activate occurrences that can change our circumstances and situations. As we continue in deep prayers in the spirit, our spirits experiences an intercourse with the Spirit of God. The oneness with the Spirit of God enables the Holy Spirit to take over and begin to intercede for us. Groaning in the spirit occurs when the Holy Spirit bares us up and takes over our prayers to God. Apostle Paul made a reference to this activity when he said, ***"Likewise the Spirit also helpeth our infirmities: for we know not what we should pray for as we ought: but the Spirit itself maketh intercession for us with groanings which cannot be uttered. [27]***

And he that searcheth the hearts knoweth what is the mind of the Spirit, because he maketh intercession for the saints according to the will of God". *Romans 8:26-27.*

When we groan in the Spirit, we cause a spiritual transaction to be initiated and consummated. Jesus demonstrated this activity at the tomb of Lazarus before raising him from the dead. ***"Then when Mary was come where Jesus was, and saw him, she fell down at his feet, saying unto him, Lord, if thou hadst been here, my brother had not died. [33] When Jesus therefore saw her weeping, and the Jews also weeping which came with her, he groaned in the spirit, and was troubled, [34] And said, Where have ye laid him? They said unto him, Lord, come and see. [35] Jesus wept. [36] Then said the Jews, Behold how he loved him! [37] And***

some of them said, Could not this man, which opened the eyes of the blind, have caused that even this man should not have died? [38] Jesus therefore again groaning in himself cometh to the grave. It was a cave, and a stone lay upon it. [39] Jesus said, Take ye away the stone. Martha, the sister of him that was dead, saith unto him, Lord, by this time he stinketh: for he hath been dead four days. [40] Jesus saith unto her, Said I not unto thee, that, if thou wouldest believe, thou shouldest see the glory of God? [41] Then they took away the stone from the place where the dead was laid. And Jesus lifted up his eyes, and said, Father, I thank thee that thou hast heard me. [42] And I knew that thou hearest me always: but because of the people which stand by I said it, that they may believe that thou hast sent me. [43] And when he thus had spoken, he

cried with a loud voice, Lazarus, come forth. [44] And he that was dead came forth, bound hand and foot with grave clothes: and his face was bound about with a napkin. Jesus saith unto them, loose him, and let him go". *John 11:32-44.*

Jesus was born into a Jewish family He grew up among Jews with strict Jewish tradition. Jews traditionally pray daily. They are well schooled in the writings of the scripture. However his disciples who also were Jews noticed something remarkable about him. They observed that he received answers to all his prayers. They realized that unlike themselves, his prayers were more effective than theirs. One of his disciples therefore asked him to teach them how to pray. ***"And it came to pass, that, as he was praying in a certain place, when he ceased, one of his disciples said unto him, Lord, teach us to***

pray, as John also taught his disciples. [2] And he said unto them, When ye pray, say, Our Father which art in heaven, Hallowed be thy name. Thy kingdom come. Thy will be done, as in heaven, so in earth. [3] Give us day by day our daily bread. [4] And forgive us our sins; for we also forgive every one that is indebted to us. And lead us not into temptation; but deliver us from evil". *Luke 11:1-4.*

During his various teachings, Jesus taught his followers how to make their prayers effective. Jesus said to pray for their enemies, ***"Ye have heard that it hath been said, Thou shalt love thy neighbour, and hate thine enemy. [44] But I say unto you, Love your enemies, bless them that curse you, do good to them that hate you, and pray for them which despitefully use you, and persecute you; [45] That ye may be the***

children of your Father which is in heaven: for he maketh his sun to rise on the evil and on the good, and sendeth rain on the just and on the unjust. [46] For if ye love them which love you, what reward have ye? Do not even the publicans the **same?"** *Matthew 5:43-46.*

Jesus taught his disciples not to make a public show of their prayers by making long speeches or praying publicly to be praised by men, ***"And when thou prayest, thou shalt not be as the hypocrites are: for they love to pray standing in the synagogues and in the corners of the streets, that they may be seen of men. Verily I say unto you, They have their reward. [6] But thou, when thou prayest, enter into thy closet, and when thou hast shut thy door, pray to thy Father which is in secret; and thy Father which seeth in secret shall reward thee openly. [7] But***

when ye pray, use not vain repetitions, as the heathen do : for they think that they shall be heard for their much speaking. [8] Be not ye therefore like unto them: for your Father knoweth what things ye have need of, before ye ask him". *Matthew 6:5-8.*

Jesus taught his disciples to pray for the salvation of souls and for ministers of the gospel, ***"And Jesus went about all the cities and villages, teaching in their synagogues, and preaching the gospel of the kingdom, and healing every sickness and every disease among the people. [36] But when he saw the multitudes, he was moved with compassion on them, because they fainted, and were scattered abroad, as sheep having no shepherd. [37] Then saith he unto his disciples, The harvest truly is plenteous, but the labourers are few; [38] Pray***

ye therefore the Lord of the harvest, that he will send forth labourers into his harvest".

Matthew 9:35-38.

The lord Jesus instructed his disciples to add fasting to their prayers when dealing with stubborn situations caused by unbelief. A case was recorded in the gospel of Matthew. ***"And when they were come to the multitude, there came to him a certain man, kneeling down to him, and saying, [15] Lord, have mercy on my son: for he is lunatick, and sore vexed: for ofttimes he falleth into the fire, and oft into the water. [16] And I brought him to thy disciples, and they could not cure him. [17] Then Jesus answered and said, O faithless and perverse generation, how long shall I be with you? How long shall I suffer you? Bring him hither to me. [18] And Jesus rebuked the devil; and he***

departed out of him: and the child was cured from that very hour. [19] Then came the disciples to Jesus apart, and said, why could not we cast him out? [20] And Jesus said unto them, Because of your unbelief: for verily I say unto you, If ye have faith as a grain of mustard seed, ye shall say unto this mountain, Remove hence to yonder place; and it shall remove; and nothing shall be impossible unto you".

Matthew 17:14-20.

Jesus clearly identified unbelief as the primary reason why God's children are unable to handle adverse situations around them. To deal with unbelief, Jesus instructs that we must fast and pray. Unbelief short-circuits the power of God in our lives. It renders God's children powerless and ineffective in the face of adverse situations and circumstances. The cure for unbelief is a voracious study of God's word with intense prayers and fasting. Our belief in God and his word is founded on our faith in his word. How do we receive faith? Apostle Paul provided the answer when he said, ***"So then faith cometh by hearing, and hearing by the word of God"*** *Romans 10:17.*

This means that the more of God's word we study, hear and receive, the greater our faith. Emphasizing the importance of faith when we pray, Matthew recorded an important incident during the ministry of Jesus on the Earth. ***"Now in the morning as he returned into the city, he hungered. [19] And when he saw a fig tree in the way, he came to it, and found nothing thereon, but leaves only, and said unto it, Let no fruit grow on thee henceforward for ever. And presently the fig tree withered away. [20] And***

when the disciples saw it, they marvelled, saying, How soon is the fig tree withered away! [21] Jesus answered and said unto them, Verily I say unto you, If ye have faith, and doubt not, ye shall not only do this which is done to the fig tree, but also if ye shall say unto this mountain, Be thou removed, and be thou cast into the sea; it shall be done. [22] And all things, whatsoever ye shall ask in prayer, believing, ye shall receive". *Matthew 21:18-22.*

The lord emphasized the importance of forgiveness when we pray. ***"And when ye stand praying, forgive, if ye have ought against any: that your Father also which is in heaven may forgive you your trespasses. [26] But if ye do not forgive, neither will your Father which is in heaven forgive your trespasses".***

Mark 11:25-26.

We can observe for the scripture above, that unforgiveness is one of the major reasons why our prayers are not answered by God. Jesus admonished his disciples to pray especially in times of trials, temptations and tribulations. A clear example was before his passion and death. He said something very significant to Peter, one of his disciples, ***"And the Lord said, Simon, Simon, behold, Satan hath desired to have you, that he may sift you as wheat: [32] But I have prayed for thee, that thy faith fail not: and when thou art converted, strengthen thy brethren".*** *Luke 22:31-32.*

The most important ingredient in prayer is to pray the right way. Jesus instructed his followers to pray in his name. He said, ***"Verily, verily, I say unto you, He that believeth on me,***

the works that I do shall he do also; and greater works than these shall he do; because I go unto my Father. [13] And whatsoever ye shall ask in my name, that will I do, that the Father may be glorified in the Son. [14] If ye shall ask any thing in my name, I will do it". *John 14:12-14.*

Emphasizing this very important point Jesus said, ***"And in that day ye shall ask me nothing. Verily, verily, I say unto you, Whatsoever ye shall ask the Father in my name, he will give it you. [24] Hitherto have ye asked nothing in my name: ask, and ye shall receive, that your joy may be full".*** *John 16:23-24.*

Furthermore he said, "At that day ye shall ask in my name: and I say not unto you, that I will pray the Father for you: [27] For the Father himself loveth you, because ye have loved me, and have believed that I came out from

God". *John 16:26-27.*

Jesus prayed for the church. As recorded in the gospel of John, The lord referred to the church in his prayer when he said, ***"I pray for them: I pray not for the world, but for them which thou hast given me; for they are thine. [15] I pray not that thou shouldest take them out of the world, but that thou shouldest keep them from the evil. [20] Neither pray I for these alone, but for them also which shall believe on me through their word"*** *John 17:9,15, 20.*

In the gospel of Luke, the bible recorded a parable made by Jesus encouraging men to pray always. ***"And he spake a parable unto them to this end , that men ought always to pray, and not to faint; [2] Saying, There was in a city a judge, which feared not God, neither regarded man:***

[3] And there was a widow in that city; and she came unto him, saying, Avenge me of mine adversary. [4] And he would not for a while: but afterward he said within himself, Though I fear not God, nor regard man; [5] Yet because this widow troubleth me, I will avenge her, lest by her continual coming she weary me. [6] And the Lord said, Hear what the unjust judge saith. [7] And shall not God avenge his own elect, which cry day and night unto him, though he bear long with them? [8] I tell you that he will avenge them speedily. Nevertheless when the Son of man cometh, shall he find faith on the earth?"

Luke 18:1-8.

5

COMPASSIONATE

All through his ministry on Earth, the Lord Jesus showed a deep sense of sympathetic consciousness of the people's challenges with a genuine desire to alleviate them. In the gospel of Mark, the bible recorded, ***"And Jesus, when he came out, saw much people, and was moved with compassion toward them, because they were as sheep not having a shepherd: and he began to teach them many things"***. *Mark 6:34.*

After teaching them, Jesus refused to send them away instead, he miraculously blessed and turned five loaves of bread and two fishes to a meal for five thousand men. They had a leftover of twelve baskets full of fragments and fishes after the meal. His compassion triggered the miraculous occurrence during the meeting. A compassionate heart is the most vital ingredient for evangelism and soul winning. The bible recorded in the gospel of Matthew, ***"And Jesus went about all the cities and villages, teaching in their synagogues, and preaching the gospel of the kingdom, and healing every sickness and every disease among the people. [36] But when he saw the multitudes, he was moved with compassion on them, because they fainted, and were scattered abroad, as sheep having no shepherd. [37] Then saith he unto his disciples, The harvest truly is plenteous, but the labourers are few; [38] Pray ye therefore the Lord of the harvest, that he will send forth labourers into his harvest".*** *Matthew 9:35-38.*

His compassion for souls led Jesus to ask that we pray for ministers and missionaries of the gospel. A heart of compassion is required for effective prayers for lost souls and effective ministry in God's vineyard. To deal with unforgiveness, we require a heart of compassion. Jesus painted a beautiful picture of this principle in a story, ***"Then came Peter to him, and said, Lord, how oft shall my brother sin against me, and I forgive him? Till seven times? [22] Jesus saith unto him, I say not unto thee, Until seven times: but, Until seventy times seven. [23] Therefore is the kingdom of heaven likened unto a certain king, which would take account of his servants. [24] And when he had begun to reckon, one was brought unto him, which owed him ten thousand talents. [25] But forasmuch as he had not to pay, his lord commanded him to be***

sold, and his wife, and children, and all that he had, and payment to be made. [26] The servant therefore fell down, and worshipped him, saying, Lord, have patience with me, and I will pay thee all. [27] Then the lord of that servant was moved with compassion, and loosed him, and forgave him the debt. [28] But the same servant went out, and found one of his fellow servants, which owed him an hundred pence: and he laid hands on him, and took him by the throat, saying, Pay me that thou owest. [29] And his fellow servant fell down at his feet, and besought him, saying, Have patience with me, and I will pay thee all. [30] And he would not: but went and cast him into prison, till he should pay the debt. [31] So when his fellow servants saw what was done, they were very sorry, and came and told unto their lord all that was done.

[32] Then his lord, after that he had called him, said unto him, O thou wicked servant, I forgave thee all that debt, because thou desiredst me: [33] Shouldest not thou also have had compassion on thy fellow servant, even as I had pity on thee? [34] And his lord was wroth, and delivered him to the tormentors, till he should pay all that was due unto him. [35] So likewise shall my heavenly Father do also unto you, if ye from your hearts forgive not every one his brother their trespasses". *Matthew 18:21-35*

Most of his healing miracles were triggered by his compassionate heart. Jesus healed two blind men because of his compassion for them, ***"And as they departed from Jericho, a great multitude followed him. [30] And, behold, two blind men sitting by the way side, when they heard that Jesus passed by, cried out, saying,***

Have mercy on us, O Lord, thou Son of David. [31] And the multitude rebuked them, because they should hold their peace: but they cried the more, saying, Have mercy on us, O Lord, thou Son of David. [32] And Jesus stood still, and called them, and said, What will ye that I shall do unto you? [33] They say unto him, Lord, that our eyes may be opened. [34] So Jesus had compassion on them, and touched their eyes: and immediately their eyes received sight, and they followed him". *Matthew 20:29-34.*

A heart of compassion is superior to any law or rules governing men. Jesus demonstrated this principle in the following incident. ***"And he preached in their synagogues throughout all Galilee, and cast out devils. [40] And there came a leper to him, beseeching him, and kneeling down to him, and saying unto him, If thou wilt,***

thou canst make me clean. [41] And Jesus, moved with compassion, put forth his hand, and touched him, and saith unto him, I will; be thou clean. [42] And as soon as he had spoken, immediately the leprosy departed from him, and he was cleansed". *Mark 1:39-42.*

Leprosy is a terrible affliction which makes the victim an outcast from the people. A leper must not touch or associate with other members of the society. Jesus defied this law when he touched the leprous. Rather than being defiled, Jesus cleansed the man from his affliction. The power to cleanse the leprous was activated by the force of compassion in the heart of the Lord Jesus. Compassion is a force that activates the power of God to work in our lives and circumstances. It lifts an individual from the carnal to the supernatural, causing him to act in the place of God. The bible tells a beautiful story of how the Lord cast out demons from a man in the country of the Gadarenes. ***"And they came over unto the other side of the sea, into the country of the Gadarenes. [2] And when he was come out of the ship, immediately there met him out of the tombs a man with an unclean spirit, [3] Who had his dwelling among the tombs; and no man could bind him, no, not with chains: [4] Because that he had been often bound with fetters and chains, and the chains had been plucked asunder by him, and the fetters broken in pieces: neither could any man tame him. [5] And always, night and day, he was in the mountains, and in the tombs, crying, and cutting himself with stones. [6] But when he saw Jesus afar off, he ran and worshipped him, [7] And cried with a loud voice, and said, What have***

I to do with thee, Jesus, thou Son of the most high God? I adjure thee by God, that thou torment me not. [8] For he said unto him, Come out of the man, thou unclean spirit. [9] And he asked him, What is thy name? And he answered, saying, My name is Legion: for we are many. [10] And he besought him much that he would not send them away out of the country. [11] Now there was there nigh unto the mountains a great herd of swine feeding. [12] And all the devils besought him, saying, Send us into the swine, that we may enter into them. [13] And forthwith Jesus gave them leave. And the unclean spirits went out, and entered into the swine: and the herd ran violently down a steep place into the sea, (they were about two thousand) and were choked in the sea. [14] And they that fed the swine fled, and told it in the city, and in the

country. And they went out to see what it was that was done. [15] And they come to Jesus, and see him that was possessed with the devil, and had the legion, sitting, and clothed, and in his right mind: and they were afraid. [16] And they that saw it told them how it befell to him that was possessed with the devil, and also concerning the swine. [17] And they began to pray him to depart out of their coasts. [18] And when he was come into the ship, he that had been possessed with the devil prayed him that he might be with him. [19] Howbeit Jesus suffered him not, but saith unto him, Go home to thy friends, and tell them how great things the Lord hath done for thee, and hath had compassion on thee. [20] And he departed, and began to publish in Decapolis how great things Jesus had done for him: and all men did marvel". *Mark 5:1-20.*

The compassion of Jesus brought deliverance to the man possessed by devils and turned him into a great evangelist, glory to God! Compassion can alter the cause of nature and change circumstances in our favour. This was demonstrated by Jesus when he raised a widow's son at Nain from the dead. ***"And it came to pass the day after, that he went into a city called Nain; and many of his disciples went with him, and much people. [12] Now when he came nigh to the gate of the city, behold, there was a dead man carried out, the only son of his mother, and she was a widow: and much people of the city was with her. [13] And when the Lord saw her, he had compassion on her, and said unto her, Weep not. [14] And he came and touched the bier: and they that bare him stood still. And he said, Young man, I say unto thee, Arise. [15] And he that was***

dead sat up, and began to speak. And he delivered him to his mother". *Luke 7:11-15.*

Compassion makes us spiritual conduits, equipped to transmit the power of God to cause changes in the lives of others. Jesus told a beautiful story to illustrate the effect of compassion, ***"And Jesus answering said, A certain man went down from Jerusalem to Jericho, and fell among thieves, which stripped him of his raiment, and wounded him, and departed, leaving him half dead. [31] And by chance there came down a certain priest that way: and when he saw him, he passed by on the other side. [32] And likewise a Levite, when he was at the place, came and looked on him, and passed by on the other side. [33] But a certain Samaritan, as he journeyed, came where he was: and when he saw him, he had compassion***

on him, [34] And went to him, and bound up his wounds, pouring in oil and wine, and set him on his own beast, and brought him to an inn, and took care of him. [35] And on the morrow when he departed, he took out two pence, and gave them to the host, and said unto him, Take care of him; and whatsoever thou spendest more, when I come again, I will repay thee. [36] Which now of these three, thinkest thou, was neighbour unto him that fell among the thieves ?"

Luke 10:30-36.

Compassion is the true test of God's love in our hearts. Apostle John in his epistle to the churches wrote, ***"Hereby perceive we the love of God, because he laid down his life for us: and we ought to lay down our lives for the brethren. [17] But whoso hath this world's good, and seeth his brother have need, and shutteth up his bowels of***

compassion from him, how dwelleth the love of God in him? [18] My little children let us not love in word, neither in tongue; but in deed and in truth". *1 John 3:16-18.*

A heart of Compassion is not quick to judge and never condemns. Jesus illustrated this in the following incident, ***"And the scribes and Pharisees brought unto him a woman taken in adultery; and when they had set her in the midst, [4] They say unto him, Master, this woman was taken in adultery, in the very act. [5] Now Moses in the law commanded us, that such should be stoned: but what sayest thou? [6] This they said, tempting him that they might have to accuse him. But Jesus stooped down, and with his finger wrote on the ground, as though he heard them not. [7] So when they continued asking him, he lifted up himself, and said unto them,***

He that is without sin among you, let him first cast a stone at her. [8] And again he stooped down, and wrote on the ground. [9] And they which heard it , being convicted by their own conscience, went out one by one, beginning at the eldest, even unto the last: and Jesus was left alone, and the woman standing in the midst. [10] When Jesus had lifted up himself, and saw none but the woman, he said unto her, Woman, where are those thine accusers? Hath no man condemned thee? [11] She said, No man, Lord. And Jesus said unto her, Neither do I condemn thee: go, and sin no more" *John 8:3-11.*

Compassion transcends the limitations of religion. Some of God's children are held bound by the tenets and doctrines of religion and as such are unable to live and enjoy the benefits of their source and callings. In some instances, Jesus defied the doctrines of the religious affiliations and released people from their bonds, restoring them to their God ordained destinies. A few of the instances are listed below: ***"And he was teaching in one of the synagogues on the Sabbath. [11] And, behold, there was a woman which had a spirit of infirmity eighteen years, and was bowed together, and could in no wise lift up herself. [12] And when Jesus saw her, he called her to him, and said unto her, Woman, thou art loosed from thine infirmity. [13] And he laid his hands on her: and immediately she was made straight, and glorified God. [14] And the ruler of the synagogue answered with indignation, because that Jesus had healed on the Sabbath day, and said unto the people, There are six days in which men ought to work: in them therefore come and be healed, and not on the Sabbath day. [15] The***

Lord then answered him, and said, Thou hypocrite, doth not each one of you on the Sabbath loose his ox or his ass from the stall, and lead him away to watering? [16] And ought not this woman, being a daughter of Abraham, whom Satan hath bound, lo, these eighteen years, be loosed from this bond on the Sabbath day? And when he said these things, all his adversaries were ashamed: and all the people rejoiced for all the glorious things that were done by him" *Luke 13:10-17.*

"And it came to pass also on another Sabbath, that he entered into the synagogue and taught: and there was a man whose right hand was withered. [7] And the scribes and Pharisees watched him, whether he would heal on the Sabbath day; that they might find an accusation against him. [8] But he knew their thoughts, and

said to the man which had the withered hand, Rise up, and stand forth in the midst. And he arose and stood forth. [9] Then said Jesus unto them, I will ask you one thing; Is it lawful on the Sabbath days to do good, or to do evil? To save life, or to destroy it? [10] And looking round about upon them all, he said unto the man, Stretch forth thy hand. And he did so: and his hand was restored whole as the other. [11] And they were filled with madness; and communed one with another what they might do to Jesus". *Luke 6:6-11.*

Another of such incident was recorded in the gospel of John. ***"Now there is at Jerusalem by the sheep market a pool, which is called in the Hebrew tongue Bethesda, having five porches. [3] In these lay a great multitude of impotent folk, of blind, halt, withered, waiting for the***

moving of the water. [4] For an angel went down at a certain season into the pool, and troubled the water: whosoever then first after the troubling of the water stepped in was made whole of whatsoever disease he had. [5] And a certain man was there, which had an infirmity thirty and eight years. [6] When Jesus saw him lie, and knew that he had been now a long time in that case , he saith unto him, Wilt thou be made whole? [7] The impotent man answered him, Sir, I have no man, when the water is troubled, to put me into the pool: but while I am coming, another steppeth down before me. [8] Jesus saith unto him, Rise, take up thy bed, and walk. [9] And immediately the man was made whole, and took up his bed, and walked: and on the same day was the Sabbath. [10] The Jews therefore said unto him that was cured, It is the

Sabbath day: it is not lawful for thee to carry thy bed. [11] He answered them, He that made me whole, the same said unto me, Take up thy bed, and walk. [12] Then asked they him, what man is that which said unto thee, Take up thy bed, and walk? [13] And he that was healed wist not who it was: for Jesus had conveyed himself away, a multitude being in that place. [14] Afterward Jesus findeth him in the temple, and said unto him, Behold, thou art made whole: sin no more, lest a worse thing come unto thee. [15] The man departed, and told the Jews that it was Jesus, which had made him whole. [16] And therefore did the Jews persecute Jesus, and sought to slay him, because he had done these things on the Sabbath day". *John 5:2-16.*

6

PASSION FOR GOD AND HIS KINGDOM

All through his days on Earth, Jesus lived a life marked by a genuine passion for God and his kingdom. While teaching in one occasion, he was asked what the greatest commandment was, ***"Then one of them, which was a lawyer, asked him a question, tempting him, and saying, [36] Master, which is the great commandment in the law? [37] Jesus said unto him, Thou shalt love the Lord thy God with all thy heart, and with all thy soul, and with all thy mind. [38] This is the first and great commandment".***

Matthew 22:35-38.

Jesus teaches us from the scripture above that man's greatest duty and responsibility is to love God completely without reservations. This should be the motivation and driving force behind every decision and action of man. At the beginning of his ministry, Jesus defined his purpose, when he read from the book of Isaiah, ***"And he came to Nazareth, where he had been brought up: and, as his custom was, he went into the synagogue on the sabbath day, and stood up for to read. [17] And there was delivered unto him the book of the prophet Esaias. And when he had opened the book, he found the place where it was written, [18] The Spirit of the Lord is upon me, because he hath anointed me to preach the gospel to the poor; he hath sent me to heal the brokenhearted, to preach deliverance to the captives, and recovering of sight to the blind,***

to set at liberty them that are bruised, [19] To preach the acceptable year of the Lord. [20] And he closed the book, and he gave it again to the minister, and sat down. And the eyes of all them that were in the synagogue were fastened on him. [21] And he began to say unto them, This day is this scripture fulfilled in your ears". *Luke 4:16-21.*

Jesus was bold enough to say that he has come to fulfill scripture. The reason and purpose of his coming was to do the will of God. While dealing with man's issues and concerns, Jesus provided a perfect solution for the needs man, He said, ***"Therefore take no thought, saying, What shall we eat? or, What shall we drink? or, Wherewithal shall we be clothed? [32] (For after all these things do the Gentiles seek) for your heavenly Father knoweth that ye have***

need of all these things. [33] But seek ye first the kingdom of God, and his righteousness; and all these things shall be added unto you".
Matthew 6:31-33.

This account was also repeated in the gospel of Luke 12:31. Jesus clearly stated that our priority should be the advancement of God's kingdom and God's righteousness. These would guarantee the attainment of a fulfilled life on Earth. His passion for God and his kingdom was revealed in every detail of his life. When his disciples asked him to teach them how to pray, he did teach, ***"And it came to pass, that, as he was praying in a certain place, when he ceased, one of his disciples said unto him, Lord, teach us to pray, as John also taught his disciples. [2] And he said unto them, When ye pray, say, Our Father which art in heaven, Hallowed be thy***

***name. Thy kingdom come. Thy will be done, as in heaven, so in earth". ****Luke 11:1-2.*

Jesus taught us to pray for the establishment of God's kingdom on Earth. He instructed us also to pray for the performance of God's will on Earth as it is done in heaven. Genuine passion for God makes us willing tools in the hands of the master. He is able to channel his power and grace through us to our ailing world. Our passion for God makes us God's outstretched arms to the sick and the needy on Earth. We are thus transformed to gods on Earth. As we step into his place, we are able to make changes and restore order and peace on Earth. It is our responsibility to make the right choice of serving God with a passionate heart and make his kingdom our priority. A particular encounter happened between Jesus a young rich ruler, it was recorded that ***"And a certain ruler asked him, saying, Good Master, what shall I do to inherit eternal life? [19] And Jesus said unto him, Why callest thou me good? None is good, save one, that is, God. [20] Thou knowest the commandments, Do not commit adultery, Do not kill, Do not steal, Do not bear false witness, Honour thy father and thy mother. [21] And he said, All these have I kept from my youth up. [22] Now when Jesus heard these things, he said unto him, Yet lackest thou one thing: sell all that thou hast, and distribute unto the poor, and thou shalt have treasure in heaven: and come, follow me. [23] And when he heard this, he was very sorrowful: for he was very rich".*** *Luke 18:18-23.*

It is important to note as we see from the scripture above that the Lord does not expect us to allow anything to stand between us and him. As we walk with God, we realize that the reason for all we receive from him is primarily for our service to him. All he has given us is for his service. We are only custodians of his wealth and riches. Our hearts must continually be stayed on him and not distracted by the materials of this world. In Matthew's account of the same encounter, he recorded Jesus as saying, ***"Jesus said unto him, If thou wilt be perfect, go and sell that thou hast, and give to the poor, and thou shalt have treasure in heaven: and come and follow me".*** *Matthew 19:21.*

Emphasizing this point Jesus said, ***"Lay not up for yourselves treasures upon earth, where moth and rust doth corrupt, and where thieves break through and steal: [20] But lay up for yourselves treasures in heaven, where neither moth nor rust doth corrupt, and where***

thieves do not break through nor steal: [21] For where your treasure is, there will your heart be also". *Matthew 6:19-21.*

Affirming the benefits of kingdom service, Jesus revealed the following, ***"Then Peter said, Lo, we have left all, and followed thee. [29] And he said unto them, Verily I say unto you, There is no man that hath left house, or parents, or brethren, or wife, or children, for the kingdom of God's sake, [30] Who shall not receive manifold more in this present time, and in the world to come life everlasting".*** *Luke 18:28-30.*

Jesus vividly described the level of passion required for kingdom service when he said, ***"For whosoever will save his life shall lose it; but whosoever shall lose his life for my sake and the gospel's, the same shall save it. [36] For what shall it profit a man, if he shall gain the whole***

world, and lose his own soul? [37] Or what shall a man give in exchange for his soul? [38] Whosoever therefore shall be ashamed of me and of my words in this adulterous and sinful generation; of him also shall the Son of man be ashamed, when he cometh in the glory of his Father with the holy angels". *Mark 8:35-38.*

Jesus painted a beautiful picture in a parable concerning our commitment to him or being distracted by earthly riches. ***"And he spake a parable unto them, saying, The ground of a certain rich man brought forth plentifully: [17] And he thought within himself, saying, What shall I do, because I have no room where to bestow my fruits? [18] And he said, This will I do: I will pull down my barns, and build greater; and there will I bestow all my fruits and my goods. [19] And I will say to my soul, Soul, thou***

hast much goods laid up for many years; take thine ease, eat, drink, and be merry. [20] But God said unto him, Thou fool, this night thy soul shall be required of thee: then whose shall those things be, which thou hast provided? [21] So is he that layeth up treasure for himself, and is not rich toward God". *Luke 12:16-21.*

Jesus emphasized the importance of making the right choice and the consequence of doing otherwise when he said, ***"And if thy right eye offend thee, pluck it out, and cast it from thee: for it is profitable for thee that one of thy members should perish, and not that thy whole body should be cast into hell. [30] And if thy right hand offend thee, cut it off, and cast it from thee: for it is profitable for thee that one of thy members should perish, and not that thy whole body should be cast into hell".*** *Matthew 5:29-30.*

Jesus revealed the easiest way to have and maintain a burning passion for God and his kingdom. This according to him is through uninterrupted fellowship with him and his words. The bible provided an illustration of this principle in the following story, ***"Now it came to pass, as they went, that he entered into a certain village: and a certain woman named Martha received him into her house. [39] And she had a sister called Mary, which also sat at Jesus' feet, and heard his word. [40] But Martha was cumbered about much serving, and came to him, and said, Lord, dost thou not care that my sister hath left me to serve alone? bid her therefore that she help me. [41] And Jesus answered and said unto her, Martha, Martha, thou art careful and troubled about many things: [42] But one thing is needful: and Mary hath chosen that good***

part, which shall not be taken away from her."
Luke 10:38-42.

Passion for God and his kingdom triggers favor from God. Luke told a beautiful story about a Centurion who, though not a Jew, loved God and his kingdom. He built a Synagogue, a place of worship for the people of God. ***"Now when he had ended all his sayings in the audience of the people, he entered into Capernaum. [2] And a certain centurion's servant, who was dear unto him, was sick, and ready to die. [3] And when he heard of Jesus, he sent unto him the elders of the Jews, beseeching him that he would come and heal his servant. [4] And when they came to Jesus, they besought him instantly, saying, That he was worthy for whom he should do this: [5] For he loveth our nation, and he hath built us a***

synagogue. [6] Then Jesus went with them. And when he was now not far from the house, the centurion sent friends to him, saying unto him, Lord, trouble not thyself: for I am not worthy that thou shouldest enter under my roof: [7] Wherefore neither thought I myself worthy to come unto thee: but say in a word, and my servant shall be healed. [8] For I also am a man set under authority, having under me soldiers, and I say unto one, Go, and he goeth; and to another, Come, and he cometh; and to my servant, Do this, and he doeth it. [9] When Jesus heard these things, he marvelled at him, and turned him about, and said unto the people that followed him, I say unto you, I have not found so great faith, no, not in Israel. [10] And they that were sent, returning to the house, found the servant whole that had been sick". *Luke 7:1-10.*

7

RESPONSIBLE

The lord Jesus has a very deep sense of responsibility. This was demonstrated by his unalloyed commitment for the welfare of his followers. In the gospel of John, he said, ***"I am the good shepherd: the good shepherd giveth his life for the sheep. [12] But he that is an hireling, and not the shepherd, whose own the sheep are not, seeth the wolf coming, and leaveth the sheep, and fleeth: and the wolf catcheth them, and scattereth the sheep. [13] The hireling fleeth, because he is an hireling, and careth not for the sheep. [14] I am the good shepherd, and know my sheep, and am known of mine".***

John 10:11-14.

Matthew recorded an important incident during the life of Christ on Earth. ***"And Jesus departed from thence, and came nigh unto the sea of Galilee; and went up into a mountain, and sat down there. [30] And great multitudes came unto him, having with them those that were lame, blind, dumb, maimed, and many others, and cast them down at Jesus' feet; and he healed them: [31] Insomuch that the multitude wondered, when they saw the dumb to speak, the maimed to be whole, the lame to walk, and the blind to see: and they glorified the God of Israel. [32] Then Jesus called his disciples unto him , and said, I have compassion on the multitude, because they continue with me now three days, and have nothing to eat: and I will not send them away fasting, lest they faint in the way. [33] And his disciples say unto him, Whence should we***

have so much bread in the wilderness, as to fill so great a multitude? [34] And Jesus saith unto them, How many loaves have ye? And they said, Seven, and a few little fishes. [35] And he commanded the multitude to sit down on the ground. [36] And he took the seven loaves and the fishes, and gave thanks, and brake them , and gave to his disciples, and the disciples to the multitude. [37] And they did all eat, and were filled: and they took up of the broken meat that was left seven baskets full. [38] And they that did eat were four thousand men, beside women and children". *Matthew 15:29-38.*

Mark recorded another incident where Jesus acted out of a deep sense of duty and responsibility towards the people, ***"And Jesus, when he came out, saw much people, and was moved with compassion toward them, because***

they were as sheep not having a shepherd: and he began to teach them many things. [35] And when the day was now far spent, his disciples came unto him, and said, This is a desert place, and now the time is far passed: [36] Send them away, that they may go into the country round about, and into the villages, and buy themselves bread: for they have nothing to eat. [37] He answered and said unto them, Give ye them to eat. And they say unto him, Shall we go and buy two hundred pennyworth of bread, and give them to eat? [38] He saith unto them, How many loaves have ye? Go and see. And when they knew, they say, Five, and two fishes. [39] And he commanded them to make all sit down by companies upon the green grass. [40] And they sat down in ranks, by hundreds, and by fifties. [41] And when he had taken the five loaves and

the two fishes, he looked up to heaven, and blessed, and brake the loaves, and gave them to his disciples to set before them; and the two fishes divided he among them all. [42] And they did all eat, and were filled. [43] And they took up twelve baskets full of the fragments, and of the fishes. [44] And they that did eat of the loaves were about five thousand men". *Mark 6:34-44.*

Jesus showed a deep sense of responsibility. This is evidenced by his strong sense of accountability to the Father for every single soul he met while on Earth. He said, ***"All that the Father giveth me shall come to me; and him that cometh to me I will in no wise cast out. [38] For I came down from heaven, not to do mine own will, but the will of him that sent me. [39] And this is the Father's will which hath sent me, that of all which he hath given me I should***

lose nothing, but should raise it up again at the last day". *John 6:37-39.*

In his prayer to the Father for his disciples, Jesus said, ***"While I was with them in the world, I kept them in thy name: those that thou gavest me I have kept, and none of them is lost, but the son of perdition; that the scripture might be fulfilled".*** *John 17:12.*

Apostle John told a story about an incident at the beginning of Jesus' ministry. Jesus showed a deep sense of responsibility and commitment to the couple who ran out of wine during their wedding ceremony. ***"And the third day there was a marriage in Cana of Galilee; and the mother of Jesus was there: [2] And both Jesus was called, and his disciples, to the marriage. [3] And when they wanted wine, the mother of Jesus saith unto him, They have no wine. [4]***

Jesus saith unto her, Woman, what have I to do with thee? Mine hour is not yet come. [5] His mother saith unto the servants, Whatsoever he saith unto you, do it. [6] And there were set there six waterpots of stone, after the manner of the purifying of the Jews, containing two or three firkins apiece. [7] Jesus saith unto them, Fill the waterpots with water. And they filled them up to the brim. [8] And he saith unto them, Draw out now, and bear unto the governor of the feast. And they bare it. [9] When the ruler of the feast had tasted the water that was made wine, and knew not whence it was: (but the servants which drew the water knew;) the governor of the feast called the bridegroom, [10] And saith unto him, Every man at the beginning doth set forth good wine; and when men have well drunk, then that which is worse: but thou hast kept the good wine

until now". *John 2:1-10.*

Matthew told a striking story of an incident that happened after Jesus fed the five thousand men. ***"And they that had eaten were about five thousand men, beside women and children. [22] And straightway Jesus constrained his disciples to get into a ship, and to go before him unto the other side, while he sent the multitudes away. [23] And when he had sent the multitudes away, he went up into a mountain apart to pray: and when the evening was come, he was there alone. [24] But the ship was now in the midst of the sea, tossed with waves: for the wind was contrary. [25] And in the fourth watch of the night Jesus went unto them, walking on the sea. [26] And when the disciples saw him walking on the sea, they were troubled, saying, It is a spirit; and they cried out for fear. [27] But straightway Jesus***

spake unto them, saying, Be of good cheer; it is I; be not afraid. [28] And Peter answered him and said, Lord, if it be thou; bid me come unto thee on the water. [29] And he said, Come. And when Peter was come down out of the ship, he walked on the water, to go to Jesus. [30] But when he saw the wind boisterous, he was afraid; and beginning to sink, he cried, saying, Lord, save me. [31] And immediately Jesus stretched forth his hand, and caught him, and said unto him, O thou of little faith, wherefore didst thou doubt? [32] And when they were come into the ship, the wind ceased". *Matthew 14:21-32.*

That was amazing! If the Lord had not immediately stretched his hand to catch Peter, he would have drowned. The Lord would have been forced to either conduct a funeral or raise Peter from the dead. His deep sense of responsibility for Peter led him to intervene and rescue him. While on the cross of Calvary before his death, Jesus displayed a strong sense of responsibility towards his mother. He handed his mother Mary to one of his most trusted disciples, John to take care of. ***"Now there stood by the cross of Jesus his mother, and his mother's sister, Mary the wife of Cleophas, and Mary Magdalene. [26] When Jesus therefore saw his mother, and the disciple standing by, whom he loved, he saith unto his mother, Woman, behold thy son! [27] Then saith he to the disciple, Behold thy mother! And from that hour that disciple took her unto his own home".*** *John 19:25-27.*

The Apostle John recorded one remarkable encounter with Jesus after his death and resurrection. ***"There were together Simon Peter, and Thomas called Didymus, and Nathanael of***

Cana in Galilee, and the sons of Zebedee, and two other of his disciples. [3] Simon Peter saith unto them, I go a fishing. They say unto him, We also go with thee. They went forth, and entered into a ship immediately; and that night they caught nothing. [4] But when the morning was now come, Jesus stood on the shore: but the disciples knew not that it was Jesus. [5] Then Jesus saith unto them, Children, have ye any meat? They answered him, No. [6] And he said unto them, Cast the net on the right side of the ship, and ye shall find. They cast therefore, and now they were not able to draw it for the multitude of fishes. [7] Therefore that disciple whom Jesus loved saith unto Peter, It is the Lord. Now when Simon Peter heard that it was the Lord, he girt his fisher's coat unto him , (for he was naked,) and did cast himself into the sea.

[8] And the other disciples came in a little ship; (for they were not far from land, but as it were two hundred cubits,) dragging the net with fishes. [9] As soon then as they were come to land, they saw a fire of coals there, and fish laid thereon, and bread".

John 21:2-9.

After his death, his disciples were confused and distressed. Not knowing what to do next, they decided to return to their earlier trade: fishing. The Lord, mindful of their circumstance and frustration, appeared to them. By miraculously helping them catch fishes after they had toiled all night unsuccessfully, he got their attention. When they got to shore, he had a hot meal waiting for them. He proved to them that he is willing and able to appreciate and meet their needs. His deep sense of responsibility towards them motivated them to trust and follow him. Before his departure, he engaged Peter in a thought provoking conversation. This was to give Peter some clarity of purpose and deep sense of responsibility for his followers. ***"So when they had dined, Jesus saith to Simon Peter, Simon, son of Jonas, lovest thou me more than these? He saith unto him, Yea, Lord; thou knowest that I love thee. He saith unto him, Feed my lambs. [16] He saith to him again the second time, Simon, son of Jonas, lovest thou me? He saith unto him, Yea, Lord; thou knowest that I love thee. He saith unto him, Feed my sheep. [17] He saith unto him the third time, Simon, son of Jonas, lovest thou me? Peter was grieved because he said unto him the third time, Lovest thou me?***

And he said unto him, Lord, thou knowest all things; thou knowest that I love thee. Jesus saith unto him, Feed my sheep". *John 21:15-17*

8

PURPOSEFUL

All through his life on Earth, the Lord Jesus had a very clear purpose. Every step he took was aimed at achieving his God given purpose on Earth. At the age of twelve he was already fired up to pursue his purpose. ***"And when he was twelve years old, they went up to Jerusalem after the custom of the feast. [43] And when they had fulfilled the days, as they returned, the child Jesus tarried behind in Jerusalem; and Joseph and his mother knew not of it. [44] But they, supposing him to have been in the company, went a day's journey; and they sought him among their kinsfolk and acquaintance. [45] And when they found him not, they turned back***

again to Jerusalem, seeking him. [46] And it came to pass, that after three days they found him in the temple, sitting in the midst of the doctors, both hearing them, and asking them questions. [47] And all that heard him were astonished at his understanding and answers. [48] And when they saw him, they were amazed: and his mother said unto him, Son, why hast thou thus dealt with us? Behold, thy father and I have sought thee sorrowing. [49] And he said unto them, How is it that ye sought me? wist ye not that I must be about my Father's business? [50] And they understood not the saying which he spake unto them. [51] And he went down with them, and came to Nazareth, and was subject unto them: but his mother kept all these sayings in her heart". *Luke 2:42-51.*

Jesus was so focused on his assignment

that he referred to it as his food. ***"In the mean while his disciples prayed him, saying, Master, eat. [32] But he said unto them, I have meat to eat that ye know not of. [33] Therefore said the disciples one to another, Hath any man brought him ought to eat? [34] Jesus saith unto them, My meat is to do the will of him that sent me, and to finish his work".*** *John 4:31-34.*

At the beginning of his ministry, Jesus located himself in scripture and sought to fulfill it. ***"And he came to Nazareth, where he had been brought up: and, as his custom was, he went into the synagogue on the sabbath day, and stood up for to read. [17] And there was delivered unto him the book of the prophet Esaias. And when he had opened the book, he found the place where it was written, [18] The Spirit of the Lord is upon me, because he hath***

anointed me to preach the gospel to the poor; he hath sent me to heal the brokenhearted, to preach deliverance to the captives, and recovering of sight to the blind, to set at liberty them that are bruised, [19] To preach the acceptable year of the Lord. [20] And he closed the book, and he gave it again to the minister, and sat down. And the eyes of all them that were in the synagogue were fastened on him. [21] And he began to say unto them, This day is this scripture fulfilled in your ears". *Luke 4:16-21.*

Jesus clearly stated his purpose from the scripture cited above. The anointing of the Spirit upon him was for preaching the gospel to the poor, healing the brokenhearted, preaching deliverance to the captives, recovery of sight to the blind and setting at liberty, them that are bruised. This was confirmed by Jesus' response when John the Baptist sent his disciples to him. ***"Now when John had heard in the prison the works of Christ, he sent two of his disciples, [3] And said unto him, Art thou he that should come, or do we look for another? [4] Jesus answered and said unto them, Go and shew John again those things which ye do hear and see: [5] The blind receive their sight, and the lame walk, the lepers are cleansed, and the deaf hear, the dead are raised up, and the poor have the gospel preached to them. [6] And blessed is he, whosoever shall not be offended in me".*** *Matthew 11:2-6.*

During his visit to Cornelius, Peter confirmed the same scripture when he said, ***"That word, I say, ye know, which was published throughout all Judaea, and began from Galilee, after the baptism which John preached; [38]***

How God anointed Jesus of Nazareth with the Holy Ghost and with power: who went about doing good, and healing all that were oppressed of the devil; for God was with him".
Acts 10:37-38.

In fulfilling his ministry, Jesus relied solely on guidance from the God, ***"Then answered Jesus and said unto them, Verily, verily, I say unto you, The Son can do nothing of himself, but what he seeth the Father do: for what things soever he doeth, these also doeth the Son likewise. [20] For the Father loveth the Son, and sheweth him all things that himself doeth: and he will shew him greater works than these, that ye may marvel".*** *John 5:19-20.*

Jesus stated clearly that even his words are not from him but from the Father. Every word that proceeded from his lips was precise words from the Father. He said, ***"And if any man hears my words, and believe not, I judge him not: for I came not to judge the world, but to save the world. [48] He that rejecteth me, and receiveth not my words, hath one that judgeth him: the word that I have spoken, the same shall judge him in the last day. [49] For I have not spoken of myself; but the Father which sent me, he gave me a commandment, what I should say, and what I should speak. [50] And I know that his commandment is life everlasting: whatsoever I speak therefore, even as the Father said unto me, so I speak"***. *John 12:47-50.*

Jesus showed the extent of his decisiveness with regards to his purpose in the following conversation: ***"And it came to pass, that, as they went in the way, a certain man said unto him, Lord, I will follow thee whithersoever thou***

goest. [58] And Jesus said unto him, Foxes have holes, and birds of the air have nests; but the Son of man hath not where to lay his head. [59] And he said unto another, Follow me. But he said, Lord, suffer me first to go and bury my father. [60] Jesus said unto him, Let the dead bury their dead: but go thou and preach the kingdom of God. [61] And another also said, Lord, I will follow thee; but let me first go bid them farewell, which are at home at my house. [62] And Jesus said unto him, No man, having put his hand to the plough, and looking back, is fit for the kingdom of God". *Luke 9:57-62.*

Even when his life was threatened, he was not deterred for, ***"The same day there came certain of the Pharisees, saying unto him, Get thee out, and depart hence: for Herod will kill thee. [32] And he said unto them, Go ye, and tell***

that fox, Behold, I cast out devils, and I do cures today and tomorrow, and the third day I shall be perfected". *Luke 13:31-32.*

During his trial before Pilate, Jesus was unwilling to be rescued or helped by Pilate. He was more inclined to accomplishing his purpose. ***"When the chief priests therefore and officers saw him, they cried out, saying, Crucify him, crucify him. Pilate saith unto them, Take ye him, and crucify him: for I find no fault in him. [7] The Jews answered him, We have a law, and by our law he ought to die, because he made himself the Son of God. [8] When Pilate therefore heard that saying, he was the more afraid; [9] And went again into the judgment hall, and saith unto Jesus, Whence art thou? But Jesus gave him no answer. [10] Then saith Pilate unto him, Speakest thou not unto me?***

Knowest thou not that I have power to crucify thee, and have power to release thee? [11] Jesus answered, Thou couldest have no power at all against me, except it were given thee from above: therefore he that delivered me unto thee hath the greater sin. [12] And from thenceforth Pilate sought to release him: but the Jews cried out, saying, If thou let this man go, thou art not Caesar's friend: whosoever maketh himself a king speaketh against Caesar". *John 19:6-12.*

His deep sense of unalloyed purpose gave him victory over death even before his crucifixion on the cross. At the garden of Gethsemane, when he was confronted with the reality of death by crucifixion, he chose to yield himself to the will of the Father. ***"Then cometh Jesus with them unto a place called Gethsemane, and saith unto the disciples, Sit ye***

here, while I go and pray yonder. [37] And he took with him Peter and the two sons of Zebedee, and began to be sorrowful and very heavy. [38] Then saith he unto them, My soul is exceeding sorrowful, even unto death: tarry ye here, and watch with me. [39] And he went a little further, and fell on his face, and prayed, saying, O my Father, if it be possible, let this cup pass from me: nevertheless not as I will, but as thou wilt".
Matthew 26:36-39.

Since it was the ultimate will of God that he must serve as the sacrificial lamb for the redemption of man, he prayed, ***"He went away again the second time, and prayed, saying, O my Father, if this cup may not pass away from me, except I drink it, thy will be done".***
Matthew 26:42.

This incident was recorded by Mark as

follows, ***"And he went forward a little, and fell on the ground, and prayed that, if it were possible, the hour might pass from him. [36] And he said, Abba, Father, all things are possible unto thee; take away this cup from me: nevertheless not what I will, but what thou wilt".***
Mark 14:35-36.

A more vivid exposė on this incident was recorded in the book of Hebrews. ***"Who in the days of his flesh, when he had offered up prayers and supplications with strong crying and tears unto him that was able to save him from death, and was heard in that he feared; [8] Though he were a Son, yet learned he obedience by the things which he suffered; [9] And being made perfect, he became the author of eternal salvation unto all them that obey him".***

Hebrews 5:7-9

9

RESPECT FOR AUTHORITY

Throughout his days on Earth, the Lord Jesus showed unreserved respect for authority. From childhood, he was obedient to his parents, even when he knew better. A particular incident occurred when he was twelve years old. In spite of his zeal to commence his assignment he obeyed his parents. ***"And the child grew, and waxed strong in spirit, filled with wisdom: and the grace of God was upon him. [41] Now his parents went to Jerusalem every year at the feast of the Passover. [42] And when he was twelve years old, they went up to Jerusalem after the custom of the feast. [43] And when they had*** *fulfilled the days, as they returned, the child Jesus tarried behind in Jerusalem; and Joseph and his mother knew not of it. [44] But they, supposing him to have been in the company, went a day's journey; and they sought him among their kinsfolk and acquaintance. [45] And when they found him not, they turned back again to Jerusalem, seeking him. [46] And it came to pass, that after three days they found him in the temple, sitting in the midst of the doctors, both hearing them, and asking them questions. [47] And all that heard him were astonished at his understanding and answers. [48] And when they saw him, they were amazed: and his mother said unto him, Son, why hast thou thus dealt with us? Behold, thy father and I have sought thee sorrowing. [49] And he said unto them, How is it that ye sought me? wist ye*

not that I must be about my Father's business? [50] And they understood not the saying which he spake unto them. [51] And he went down with them, and came to Nazareth, and was subject unto them: but his mother kept all these sayings in her heart. [52] And Jesus increased in wisdom and stature, and in favour with God and man". *Luke 2:40-52.*

Jesus never encouraged anyone to disobey constituted authority. In one of his encounters with the Pharisees, they tried to make him speak against the authorities or encourage civil disobedience. ***"And they send unto him certain of the Pharisees and of the Herodians, to catch him in his words. [14] And when they were come, they say unto him, Master, we know that thou art true, and carest for no man: for thou regardest not the person of men, but teachest the***

way of God in truth: Is it lawful to give tribute to Caesar, or not? [15] Shall we give, or shall we not give? But he, knowing their hypocrisy, said unto them, Why tempt ye me? Bring me a penny, that I may see it . [16] And they brought it. And he saith unto them, Whose is this image and superscription? And they said unto him, Caesar's. [17] And Jesus answering said unto them, Render to Caesar the things that are Caesar's, and to God the things that are God's. And they marvelled at him". *Mark 12:13-17.*

An incident occurred which affirmed the Lord's character of respect for authority. ***"And when they were come to Capernaum, they that received tribute money came to Peter, and said, Doth not your master pay tribute? [25] He saith, Yes. And when he was come into the house, Jesus prevented him, saying, What thinkest***

thou, Simon? Of whom do the kings of the earth take custom or tribute? Of their own children, or of strangers? [26] Peter saith unto him, Of strangers. Jesus saith unto him, Then are the children free. [27] Notwithstanding, lest we should offend them, go thou to the sea, and cast an hook, and take up the fish that first cometh up; and when thou hast opened his mouth, thou shalt find a piece of money: that take, and give unto them for me and thee". *Matthew 17:24-27.*

Jesus paid his tribute. This served to correct Peter's impression in spite of his position of liberty. Before Jesus came, God gave his laws to Moses. The Prophets also made pronouncements under the inspiration of the Holy Spirit. The writings of the Laws and the Prophets are regarded as Scripture. This formed the basis for social justice and moral principles.

The children of Israel were regarded as the people of God, because they were the only group of people whose laws, rules, practices and way of life is governed by the laws of God. When Jesus came, he revealed that he did not come to destroy the law but to fulfill it. ***"Think not that I am come to destroy the law, or the prophets: I am not come to destroy, but to fulfil. [18] For verily I say unto you, Till heaven and earth pass, one jot or one title shall in no wise pass from the law, till all be fulfilled. [19] Whosoever therefore shall break one of these least commandments, and shall teach men so, he shall be called the least in the kingdom of heaven: but whosoever shall do and teach them, the same shall be called great in the kingdom of heaven".*** *Matthew 5:17-19.*

Jesus lived his life under the inspiration of the Holy Spirt. However, he took time to explain

the mind of God in the laws and showed them a better way. The Lord Jesus not only taught his disciples to have respect for authority, he went further to teach them how to handle authority. Jesus instructed them to be as servants when they are in positions of authority. ***"And there was also a strife among them, which of them should be accounted the greatest. [25] And he said unto them, The kings of the Gentiles exercise lordship over them; and they that exercise authority upon them are called benefactors. [26] But ye shall not be so: but he that is greatest among you let him be as the younger; and he that is chief, as he that doth serve".***
Luke 22:24-26.

This same account was recorded by Matthew: ***"But Jesus called them unto him, and said, Ye know that the princes of the Gentiles***

exercise dominion over them, and they that are great exercise authority upon them. [26] But it shall not be so among you: but whosoever will be great among you, let him be your minister; [27] And whosoever will be chief among you, let him be your servant: [28] Even as the Son of man came not to be ministered unto, but to minister, and to give his life a ransom for many". *Matthew 20:25-28.*

In his own account, Mark recorded similar incident as follows, ***"And he came to Capernaum: and being in the house he asked them, What was it that ye disputed among yourselves by the way? [34] But they held their peace: for by the way they had disputed among themselves, who should be the greatest. [35] And he sat down, and called the twelve, and saith unto them, If any man desire to be first, the same***

shall be last of all, and servant of all".
Mark 9:33-35.

Affirming the instructions of Christ with respect to constituted authority, Apostle Paul wrote, ***"Let every soul be subject unto the higher powers. For there is no power but of God: the powers that be are ordained of God. [2] Whosoever therefore resisteth the power, resisteth the ordinance of God: and they that resist shall receive to themselves damnation. [3] For rulers are not a terror to good works, but to the evil. Wilt thou then not be afraid of the power? Do that which is good, and thou shalt have praise of the same: [4] For he is the minister of God to thee for good. But if thou do that which is evil, be afraid; for he beareth not the sword in vain: for he is the minister of God, a revenger to execute wrath upon him that doeth***

evil. [5] Wherefore ye must needs be subject, not only for wrath, but also for conscience sake. [6] For for this cause pay ye tribute also: for they are God's ministers, attending continually upon this very thing. [7] Render therefore to all their dues: tribute to whom tribute is due; custom to whom custom; fear to whom fear; honour to whom honour". *Romans 13:1-7.*

Apostle Peter made the same assertion when he said, ***"Submit yourselves to every ordinance of man for the Lord's sake: whether it be to the king, as supreme; [14] Or unto governors, as unto them that are sent by him for the punishment of evildoers, and for the praise of them that do well. [15] For so is the will of God, that with well doing ye may put to silence the ignorance of foolish men: [16] As free, and not using your liberty for a cloke of***

maliciousness, but as the servants of God. [17] Honour all men. Love the brotherhood. Fear God. Honour the king". *1 Peter 2:13-17.*

In his letter to Titus, Apostle Paul emphasized this instruction, ***"Put them in mind to be subject to principalities and powers, to obey magistrates, to be ready to every good work".*** *Titus 3:1.*

Furthermore, in his letter to Timothy, Apostle Paul advised believers to pray earnestly for leaders, ***"I exhort therefore, that, first of all, supplications, prayers, intercessions, and giving of thanks, be made for all men; [2] For kings, and for all that are in authority; that we may lead a quiet and peaceable life in all godliness and honesty. [3] For this is good and acceptable in the sight of God our Saviour".***

1 Timothy 2:1-3.

Apostle Peter advised leaders in the house of God on how to handle authority and comport themselves. ***"The elders which are among you I exhort, who am also an elder, and a witness of the sufferings of Christ, and also a partaker of the glory that shall be revealed: [2] Feed the flock of God which is among you, taking the oversight thereof, not by constraint, but willingly; not for filthy lucre, but of a ready mind; [3] Neither as being lords over God's heritage, but being ensamples to the flock. [4] And when the chief Shepherd shall appear, ye shall receive a crown of glory that fadeth not away".*** *1 Peter 5:1-4*

10

PEACEFUL

On a certain Sabbath day, Jesus went to the Synagogue to worship. There he met a man with a withered hand. Jesus healed the man, but the Pharisees sought to kill him for healing on a Sabbath day. ***"Then the Pharisees went out, and held a council against him, how they might destroy him. [15] But when Jesus knew it, he withdrew himself from thence: and great multitudes followed him, and he healed them all; [16] And charged them that they should not make him known: [17] That it might be fulfilled which was spoken by Esaias the prophet, saying, [18] Behold my servant, whom I have chosen;***

my beloved, in whom my soul is well pleased: I will put my spirit upon him, and he shall shew judgment to the Gentiles. [19] He shall not strive, nor cry; neither shall any man hear his voice in the streets. [20] A bruised reed shall he not break, and smoking flax shall he not quench, till he send forth judgment unto victory. [21] And in his name shall the Gentiles trust". *Matthew 12:14-21.*

Apostle Matthew quoted the writings of the Prophet Isaiah concerning the Messiah. The above scripture clearly outlines the character of Jesus Christ. He is not only peaceful but he is the Prince of Peace, [Isaiah 9:6]. In fulfilling the law, he said, ***"Ye have heard that it hath been said, An eye for an eye, and a tooth for a tooth: [39] But I say unto you, That ye resist not evil: but whosoever shall smite thee on thy right cheek,***

turn to him the other also. [40] And if any man will sue thee at the law, and take away thy coat, let him have thy cloke also. [41] And whosoever shall compel thee to go a mile, go with him twain. [42] Give to him that asketh thee, and from him that would borrow of thee turn not thou away. [43] Ye have heard that it hath been said, Thou shalt love thy neighbour, and hate thine enemy. [44] But I say unto you, Love your enemies, bless them that curse you, do good to them that hate you, and pray for them which despitefully use you, and persecute you; [45] That ye may be the children of your Father which is in heaven: for he maketh his sun to rise on the evil and on the good, and sendeth rain on the just and on the unjust. [46] For if ye love them which love you, what reward have ye? Do not even the publicans the same? [47] And if ye

salute your brethren only, what do ye more than others? Do not even the publicans so? [48] Be ye therefore perfect, even as your Father which is in heaven is perfect". *Matthew 5:38-48.*

No one ever spoke like Jesus. This is the God kind of love. Only the Prince of Peace could say above words in this present evil world. This quality of peace was aptly described by Apostle Paul when he said, ***"And the peace of God, which passeth all understanding, shall keep your hearts and minds through Christ Jesus".*** *Philippians 4:7.*

This kind of peace can only come from Jesus and has been made available to every believer in Christ. Paul went further to explain how this kind of peace is sustained by the child of God. He said, ***"Finally, brethren, whatsoever things are true, whatsoever things are honest,***

whatsoever things are just, whatsoever things are pure, whatsoever things are lovely, whatsoever things are of good report; if there be any virtue, and if there be any praise, think on these things. [9] Those things, which ye have both learned, and received, and heard, and seen in me, do: and the God of peace shall be with you". *Philippians 4:8-9.*

Before his departure from the Earth, Jesus imparted his peace upon his disciples, ***"Peace I leave with you, my peace I give unto you: not as the world giveth, give I unto you. Let not your heart be troubled, neither let it be afraid".***
John 14:27.

After his resurrection from the dead, when he visited his disciples he confirmed his peace upon them, ***"Then the same day at evening, being the first day of the week, when the doors***

were shut where the disciples were assembled for fear of the Jews, came Jesus and stood in the midst, and saith unto them, Peace be unto you. [20] And when he had so said, he shewed unto them his hands and his side. Then were the disciples glad, when they saw the Lord. [21] Then said Jesus to them again, Peace be unto you: as my Father hath sent me, even so send I you". *John 20:19-21.*

When we received Christ, the Spirit of God imparts this peace to our recreated spirits. This kind of peace is enjoyed irrespective of the prevalent circumstance or situation. It is the fruit or product of the recreated human spirit. This is the peace that comes with prosperity. It is beyond human comprehension. This was the peace Christ enjoyed when he went through the gruesome ordeal in the hands of Roman soldiers.

It made him go through his passion without complaints. Even when Pilate sought to free him, he was not moved or bothered with the accusations of men. God has given us this peace to enable us deal with the storms of life. Mark recorded a significant incident in his gospel that took place on one occasion after teaching the multitude by the sea shore, ***"And the same day, when the even was come, he saith unto them, Let us pass over unto the other side. [36] And when they had sent away the multitude, they took him even as he was in the ship. And there were also with him other little ships. [37] And there arose a great storm of wind, and the waves beat into the ship, so that it was now full. [38] And he was in the hinder part of the ship, asleep on a pillow: and they awake him, and say unto him, Master, carest thou not that we perish? [39] And he***

arose, and rebuked the wind, and said unto the sea, Peace, be still. And the wind ceased, and there was a great calm. [40] And he said unto them, Why are ye so fearful? How is it that ye have no faith? [41] And they feared exceedingly, and said one to another, What manner of man is this, that even the wind and the sea obey him?" *Mark 4:35-41.*

As sons of God, we are empowered to speak peace to our lives, circumstances, families, businesses, and every other issue of concern. The same way Christ spoke peace to calm the storm we are enabled to do same. When troubles of life come to harass you, call forth the peace of God, and put the trouble under control. When you have the Prince of Peace dwelling in your heart, you must enforce that peace on your life and situation. Furthermore, we have the responsibility to enforce the peace of God in our homes and nation. We must not allow the devil to instigate chaos in our homes, neighborhood and nation. We must take charge and ensure that the peace of God reigns in our world. In one of his sermons, Jesus said, ***"Blessed are the peacemakers: for they shall be called the children of God"****. Matthew 5:9.*

This is because, ***"... God is not the author of confusion, but of peace, as in all churches of the saints"****. 1 Corinthians 14:33.*

Peter revealed the secret of increased grace and peace from God, when he said, ***"Grace and peace be multiplied unto you through the knowledge of God, and of Jesus our Lord".***
2 Peter 1:2.

Are you facing challenges in spite of your faith in God? All you need do is to put your absolute trust in Him. Yes, make up your mind to trust him. The bible says, ***"Thou wilt keep him in perfect peace, whose mind is stayed on thee: because he trusteth in thee"***. *Isaiah 26:3.*

The prophet went further to say, ***"Behold, God is my salvation; I will trust, and not be afraid: for the Lord Jehovah is my strength and my song; he also is become my salvation. [3] Therefore with joy shall ye draw water out of the wells of salvation"***. *Isaiah 12:2-3.*

In his letter to Timothy, Paul instructed that the servant of God must conduct himself peaceably in the house of God. ***"And the servant of the Lord must not strive; but be gentle unto all men, apt to teach, patient, [25] In meekness instructing those that oppose themselves; if God peradventure will give them repentance to the acknowledging of the truth"*** *2 Timothy 2:24-25.*

In order to enjoy the peace of God in our lives, the Lord Jesus taught us to forgive others when they offend us. ***"Then came Peter to him, and said, Lord, how oft shall my brother sin against me, and I forgive him? till seven times? [22] Jesus saith unto him, I say not unto thee, Until seven times: but, Until seventy times seven".*** *Matthew 18:21-22.*

It is therefore impossible to be willing to forgive each offender 490 times and fail to keep peace with such a person. The Lord also taught that unforgiveness hinders answers to prayers. ***"Therefore I say unto you, What things soever ye desire, when ye pray, believe that ye receive them, and ye shall have them. [25] And when ye stand praying, forgive, if ye have ought against any: that your Father also which is in heaven***

may forgive you your trespasses. [26] But if ye do not forgive, neither will your Father which is in heaven forgive your trespasses".
Mark 11:24-26.

At Gethsemane, Jesus healed one of his assailants, whose ear was cut off by Peter, when they were sent to arrest him. ***"And one of them smote the servant of the high priest, and cut off his right ear. [51] And Jesus answered and said, Suffer ye thus far. And he touched his ear, and healed him".*** *Luke 22:50-51.*

John threw more light on this incident when he wrote, ***"Then Simon Peter having a sword drew it, and smote the high priest's servant, and cut off his right ear. The servant's name was Malchus".*** *John 18:10.*

While hanging on the cross, with his last breath, the Lord Jesus prayed to the Father, asking

him to forgive his persecutors and assailants. ***"And when they were come to the place, which is called Calvary, there they crucified him, and the malefactors, one on the right hand, and the other on the left. [34] Then said Jesus, Father, forgive them; for they know not what they do. And they parted his raiment, and cast lots".***
Luke 23:33-34.

11

FELLOWSHIP WITH OTHER BELIEVERS

By his life and conduct while on Earth, the Lord Jesus gave us a model to live by. The bible says that he was accustomed to attending services at the Synagogue consistently. ***"And he came to Nazareth, where he had been brought up: and, as his custom was, he went into the synagogue on the Sabbath day, and stood up for to read".*** *Luke 4:16.*

The Lord Jesus made it a priority to attend prayers and services in the Synagogue. He consistently visited Jerusalem for each and every festival as required by the law. The Lord used the service times in the Synagogue to heal the sick and cast our demons. Jesus usually taught the Holy Scriptures in the Synagogues and in the temple at Jerusalem. The Lord vehemently condemned the act of carrying out trade or commercial activities in the house of God. ***"And the Jews' Passover was at hand, and Jesus went up to Jerusalem, [14] And found in the temple those that sold oxen and sheep and doves, and the changers of money sitting: [15] And when he had made a scourge of small cords, he drove them all out of the temple, and the sheep, and the oxen; and poured out the changers' money, and overthrew the tables; [16] And said unto them that sold doves, Take these things hence; make not my Father's house an house of merchandise. [17] And his disciples remembered that it was written, The zeal of thine house hath eaten me up.*** *John 2:13-17.*

The Apostle Mark reported this same incident in more explicit terms, ***"And they come to Jerusalem: and Jesus went into the temple, and began to cast out them that sold and bought in the temple, and overthrew the tables of the moneychangers, and the seats of them that sold doves; [16] And would not suffer that any man should carry any vessel through the temple. [17] And he taught, saying unto them, Is it not written, My house shall be called of all nations the house of prayer? But ye have made it a den of thieves. [18] And the scribes and chief priests heard it, and sought how they might destroy him: for they feared him, because all the people were astonished at his doctrine"***. *Mark 11:15-18.*

The Lord therefore insists that the house of God must be sacred and used solely for prayers and fellowship. The house of God is a platform for prayers, healings, studying and teaching of the word, and fellowship with other believers. The bible expressly exhorts believers never to neglect the gathering and fellowship of God's children. ***"Not forsaking the assembling of ourselves together, as the manner of some is; but exhorting one another: and so much the more, as ye see the day approaching".*** *Hebrews 10:25.*

The early Apostles and Disciples of Christ kept this very important doctrine. ***"And they, continuing daily with one accord in the temple, and breaking bread from house to house, did eat their meat with gladness and singleness of heart, [47] Praising God, and having favour with all the people. And the Lord added to the church daily such as should be saved".***
Acts 2:46-47.

The fellowship of believers provides an opportunity for the people of God to be taught God's word and to be corrected in righteousness. The assembly of believers provides guidance and leadership for the people of God. In the house of God, the children of God are prepared and equipped for life. Identifying with and staying in the company of fellow believers provides the first line of defense in the face of danger. A young believer is taught and followed-up by older or more mature believers. Questions, issues and challenges are easily handled, while in the company of fellow believers. In his letter to the Corinthians church, Apostle Paul gave a very strong warning to believers, ***"Be ye not unequally yoked together with unbelievers: for what fellowship hath righteousness with unrighteousness? And what communion hath***

light with darkness? [15] And what concord hath Christ with Belial? Or what part hath he that believeth with an infidel? [16] And what agreement hath the temple of God with idols? For ye are the temple of the living God; as God hath said, I will dwell in them, and walk in them; and I will be their God, and they shall be my people. [17] Wherefore come out from among them, and be ye separate, saith the Lord, and touch not the unclean thing ; and I will receive you, [18] And will be a Father unto you, and ye shall be my sons and daughters, saith the Lord Almighty". *2 Corinthians 6:14-18.*

Apostle John in his gospel gave an account of how Jesus visited his disciples after his resurrection. However, one of the Apostles called Thomas was not in the assembly. On his return the other Apostle told him that they have seen the risen Lord. Thomas refused to believe that Jesus has risen from the dead. His heart was filled with unbelief because he missed the Lord's visitation. He was exposed because he stayed out of fellowship and the assembly of his fellow disciples. ***"But Thomas, one of the twelve, called Didymus, was not with them when Jesus came. [25] The other disciples therefore said unto him, We have seen the Lord. But he said unto them, Except I shall see in his hands the print of the nails, and put my finger into the print of the nails, and thrust my hand into his side, I will not believe. [26] And after eight days again his disciples were within, and Thomas with them: then came Jesus, the doors being shut, and stood in the midst, and said, Peace be unto you. [27] Then saith he to Thomas, Reach hither thy finger, and behold my hands; and reach hither***

thy hand, and thrust it into my side: and be not faithless, but believing. [28] And Thomas answered and said unto him, My Lord and my God. [29] Jesus saith unto him, Thomas, because thou hast seen me, thou hast believed: blessed are they that have not seen, and yet have believed". *John 20:24-29.*

Staying away from the assembly of other disciples caused Thomas to miss the Lord's visitation and exposed him to unbelief. Although Jesus visited again and proved himself, the Lord rebuked him for his unbelief. In the book of Psalms the Psalmist said, ***"I was glad when they said unto me, Let us go into the house of the Lord".*** *Psalm 122:1.*

Emphasizing the importance of worship and fellowship in the house of God, the Psalmist said, ***"For a day in thy courts is better than a***

thousand. I had rather be a doorkeeper in the house of my God, than to dwell in the tents of wickedness". *Psalm 84:10.*

12

SPIRIT FILLED [INSPIRED]

As children of God, our inspiration must come from the Holy Spirit. Some people receive their inspiration from music, art, writings, etc. The Lord Jesus set us an example while on Earth. He was consistently filled with the Holy Spirit. Every step, choice, decision, action or response he made was inspired and directed by the Holy Spirit. In the gospel of Luke, the bible recorded that Jesus was filled with the Holy Spirit when he was baptised. The infilling of the Holy Spirit ushered him into his ministry with power. ***"Now when all the people were baptized, it came to pass, that Jesus also being baptized, and***

praying, the heaven was opened, [22] And the Holy Ghost descended in a bodily shape like a dove upon him, and a voice came from heaven, which said, Thou art my beloved Son; in thee I am well pleased". *Luke 3:21-22.*

Luke went further to say concerning the Holy Spirit upon Jesus, ***"And Jesus being full of the Holy Ghost returned from Jordan, and was led by the Spirit into the wilderness".*** *Luke 4:1.*

Isaiah the prophet spoke about the infilling of the Holy Spirit on Jesus when he said, ***"And there shall come forth a rod out of the stem of Jesse, and a Branch shall grow out of his roots: [2] And the Spirit of the LORD shall rest upon him, the spirit of wisdom and understanding, the spirit of counsel and might, the spirit of knowledge and of the fear of the LORD; [3] And shall make him of quick understanding in the***

fear of the LORD: and he shall not judge after the sight of his eyes, neither reprove after the hearing of his ears" *Isaiah 11:1-3.*

At the Synagogue during one of his days of worship, Jesus took up the scroll and read from the book of Isaiah. ***"And he came to Nazareth, where he had been brought up: and, as his custom was, he went into the synagogue on the sabbath day, and stood up for to read. [17] And there was delivered unto him the book of the prophet Esaias. And when he had opened the book, he found the place where it was written, [18] The Spirit of the Lord is upon me, because he hath anointed me to preach the gospel to the poor; he hath sent me to heal the brokenhearted, to preach deliverance to the captives, and recovering of sight to the blind, to set at liberty them that are bruised, [19] To preach the***

acceptable year of the Lord. [20] And he closed the book, and he gave it again to the minister, and sat down. And the eyes of all them that were in the synagogue were fastened on him. [21] And he began to say unto them, This day is this scripture fulfilled in your ears". *Luke 4:16-21.*

The Lord Jesus was tempted by the devil but was able to overcome the tempter with the help of the Holy Spirit. The bible says, ***"And when the devil had ended all the temptation, he departed from him for a season. [14] And Jesus returned in the power of the Spirit into Galilee: and there went out a fame of him through all the region round about.*** *Luke 4:13-14.*

Peter made a profound statement at the house of Cornelius when he was invite to share the gospel. He said, ***"The word which God sent unto the children of Israel, preaching peace by***

Jesus Christ: (he is Lord of all) [37] That word, I say, ye know, which was published throughout all Judaea, and began from Galilee, after the baptism which John preached; [38] How God anointed Jesus of Nazareth with the Holy Ghost and with power: who went about doing good, and healing all that were oppressed of the devil; for God was with him". *Acts 10:36-38.*

In his testimony concerning Jesus, John the Baptist made a significant statement about Jesus and his ministry. ***"And as the people were in expectation, and all men mused in their hearts of John, whether he were the Christ, or not; [16] John answered, saying unto them all, I indeed baptize you with water; but one mightier than I cometh, the latchet of whose shoes I am not worthy to unloose: he shall baptize you with the Holy Ghost and with fire: [17] Whose fan is***

in his hand, and he will thoroughly purge his floor, and will gather the wheat into his garner; but the chaff he will burn with fire unquenchable". *Luke 3:15-17.*

John spoke about the role of the Holy Spirit in the ministry of Jesus. Jesus was filled with the Holy Spirit and that equipped him for his ministry. John revealed that Jesus will baptize his followers with the Holy Spirit enabling them to do the work of the ministry. Talking about the infilling of the Holy Spirit on his disciples, Jesus made a remarkable statement during one of his encounters with the Pharisees, ***"In the last day, that great day of the feast, Jesus stood and cried, saying, If any man thirst, let him come unto me, and drink. [38] He that believeth on me, as the scripture hath said, out of his belly shall flow rivers of living water. [39] (But this spake he of***

the Spirit, which they that believe on him should receive: for the Holy Ghost was not yet given; because that Jesus was not yet glorified.)" *John 7:37-39.*

Introducing the Holy Spirit to his disciples, Jesus said, ***"If ye love me, keep my commandments. [16] And I will pray the Father, and he shall give you another Comforter, that he may abide with you forever; [17] Even the Spirit of truth; whom the world cannot receive, because it seeth him not, neither knoweth him: but ye know him; for he dwelleth with you, and shall be in you".*** *John 14:15-17.*

Jesus explained the role of the Holy Spirit in the lives and ministry of the disciples. ***"But the Comforter, which is the Holy Ghost, whom the Father will send in my name, he shall teach you all things, and bring all things to your***

remembrance, whatsoever I have said unto you". *John 14:26.*

He went further to say, ***"But when the Comforter is come, whom I will send unto you from the Father, even the Spirit of truth, which proceedeth from the Father, he shall testify of me: [27] And ye also shall bear witness, because ye have been with me from the beginning".*** *John 15:26-27.*

Stressing the ministry of the Holy Spirit further, Jesus said, ***"I have yet many things to say unto you, but ye cannot bear them now. [13] Howbeit when he, the Spirit of truth, is come, he will guide you into all truth: for he shall not speak of himself; but whatsoever he shall hear, that shall he speak: and he will shew you things to come. [14] He shall glorify me: for he shall receive of mine, and shall shew it unto you. [15]***

All things that the Father hath are mine: therefore said I, that he shall take of mine, and shall shew it unto you". *John 16:12-15.*

After his death and resurrection, Jesus appeared several times within a forty day period to his disciples. In one of those visits, Jesus talked about the infilling of the Holy Spirit as a vital requirement before they could embark on their ministry. ***"And, being assembled together with them, commanded them that they should not depart from Jerusalem, but wait for the promise of the Father, which, saith he, ye have heard of me. [5] For John truly baptized with water; but ye shall be baptized with the Holy Ghost not many days hence".*** *Acts 1:4-5.*

Continuing the instruction concerning the coming of the Holy Ghost, he said, ***"But ye shall receive power, after that the Holy Ghost is come***

upon you: and ye shall be witnesses unto me both in Jerusalem, and in all Judaea, and in Samaria, and unto the uttermost part of the earth". *Acts 1:8.*

Under the inspiration of the Holy Spirit, Apostle Paul revealed the acid test of the Holy Spirit in explicit terms, ***"Wherefore I give you to understand, that no man speaking by the Spirit of God calleth Jesus accursed: and that no man can say that Jesus is the Lord, but by the Holy Ghost".*** *1 Corinthians 12:3.*

The scripture above gives us a good insight about the basis for discernment of spirits. Secondly we understand that our salvation is authored and preserved by the Holy Spirit. Paul went further to say, ***"But the manifestation of the Spirit is given to every man to profit withal. [8] For to one is given by the Spirit the word of***

wisdom; to another the word of knowledge by the same Spirit; [9] To another faith by the same Spirit; to another the gifts of healing by the same Spirit; [10] To another the working of miracles; to another prophecy; to another discerning of spirits; to another divers kinds of tongues; to another the interpretation of tongues: [11] But all these worketh that one and the selfsame Spirit, dividing to every man severally as he will". *1 Corinthians 12:7-11.*

Paul revealed that the infilling of the Holy Spirit in the believer is evidenced by the manifestation of diverse spiritual gifts of: the word of wisdom, the word of knowledge, faith, healings, working of miracles, prophecy, discerning of spirits, diverse kinds of tongues, and the interpretation of tongues. Paul admonishes the believers to be filled with the spirit at all times. ***"And be not drunk with wine, wherein is excess; but be filled with the Spirit; [19] Speaking to yourselves in psalms and hymns and spiritual songs, singing and making melody in your heart to the Lord; [20] Giving thanks always for all things unto God and the Father in the name of our Lord Jesus Christ".*** *Ephesians 5:18-20.*

In his letter to the Corinthians church, Paul talked about the unveiling of the inheritance of the saints and the gifts of the Spirit. ***"But as it is written, Eye hath not seen, nor ear heard, neither have entered into the heart of man, the things which God hath prepared for them that love him. [10] But God hath revealed them unto us by his Spirit: for the Spirit searcheth all things, yea, the deep things of God. [11] For what man knoweth the things of a man, save the***

spirit of man which is in him? Even so the things of God knoweth no man, but the Spirit of God. [12] Now we have received, not the spirit of the world, but the Spirit which is of God; that we might know the things that are freely given to us of God. [13] Which things also we speak, not in the words which man's wisdom teacheth, but which the Holy Ghost teacheth; comparing spiritual things with spiritual. [14] But the natural man receiveth not the things of the Spirit of God: for they are foolishness unto him: neither can he know them, because they are spiritually discerned". *1 Corinthians 2:9-14.*

In his prayer for the church at Ephesus, Apostle Paul earnestly prayed that the Holy Spirit may cause the people of God to be stronger, more effective and fortified. ***"For this cause I bow my knees unto the Father of our Lord Jesus Christ,***

[15] of whom the whole family in heaven and earth is named, [16] That he would grant you, according to the riches of his glory, to be strengthened with might by his Spirit in the inner man". *Ephesians 3:14-16*

13

FERVENT PREACHER / TEACHER

The prophet Isaiah prophesied concerning Christ, ***"The Spirit of the Lord God is upon me; because the Lord hath anointed me to preach good tidings unto the meek; he hath sent me to bind up the brokenhearted, to proclaim liberty to the captives, and the opening of the prison to them that are bound".*** *Isaiah 61:1.*

This same scripture was recorded in the gospel of Luke as read by Jesus in a Synagogue at the beginning of his ministry, ***"And he came to Nazareth, where he had been brought up: and, as his custom was, he went into the synagogue on the sabbath day, and stood up for to read. [17]***

And there was delivered unto him the book of the prophet Esaias. And when he had opened the book, he found the place where it was written, [18] The Spirit of the Lord is upon me, because he hath anointed me to preach the gospel to the poor; he hath sent me to heal the brokenhearted, to preach deliverance to the captives, and recovering of sight to the blind, to set at liberty them that are bruised, [19] To preach the acceptable year of the Lord. [20] And he closed the book, and he gave it again to the minister, and sat down. And the eyes of all them that were in the synagogue were fastened on him. [21] And he began to say unto them, This day is this scripture fulfilled in your ears"

Luke 4:16-21.

Jesus clearly pointed out the significance of the preaching of the gospel as the antidote for poverty. ***"And John calling unto him two of his disciples sent them to Jesus, saying, Art thou he that should come? Or look we for another? [20] When the men were come unto him, they said, John Baptist hath sent us unto thee, saying, Art thou he that should come? Or look we for another? [21] And in that same hour he cured many of their infirmities and plagues, and of evil spirits; and unto many that were blind he gave sight. [22] Then Jesus answering said unto them, Go your way, and tell John what things ye have seen and heard; how that the blind see, the lame walk, the lepers are cleansed, the deaf hear, the dead are raised, to the poor the gospel is preached".*** *Luke 7:19-22.*

According to Jesus, the preaching of the gospel is the surest way to get people out of the bondage of poverty. This knowledge propelled him to focus his energy on the preaching of the gospel to liberate his people from the domain of darkness into God's kingdom of light. Before this time John the Baptist had this testimony of Jesus, ***"He that cometh from above is above all: he that is of the earth is earthly, and speaketh of the earth: he that cometh from heaven is above all. [32] And what he hath seen and heard, that he testifieth; and no man receiveth his testimony. [33] He that hath received his testimony hath set to his seal that God is true. [34] For he whom God hath sent speaketh the words of God: for God giveth not the Spirit by measure unto him".*** *John 3:31-34.*

The prophet Isaiah gave a vivid description of the ministry of Jesus when he wrote, ***"And there shall come forth a rod out of the stem of Jesse, and a Branch shall grow out of***

his roots: [2] And the Spirit of the LORD shall rest upon him, the spirit of wisdom and understanding, the spirit of counsel and might, the spirit of knowledge and of the fear of the Lord ; [3] And shall make him of quick understanding in the fear of the Lord : and he shall not judge after the sight of his eyes, neither reprove after the hearing of his ears: [4] But with righteousness shall he judge the poor, and reprove with equity for the meek of the earth: and he shall smite the earth with the rod of his mouth, and with the breath of his lips shall he slay the wicked". *Isaiah 11:1-4.*

All through his ministry on Earth, the Lord Jesus spent all his time teaching and preaching the gospel to the house of Israel. He taught his disciples to preach the gospel of the kingdom to every one they met. At every opportunity he had, he shared the gospel of the kingdom. He was called, Master, Rabbi, and Teacher because of his precise understanding of the scripture and his passion for the gospel of the kingdom of God. When he sent his disciples out to preach, he gave them power over demons and unclean spirits. He also gave them authority to heal the sick and save the lost souls in his name. Each time they went out to preach, they came back with great testimonies of healings and incidents of demons being cast out of people. Before his ascension into heaven, he charged his disciples to go forth and preach the gospel to every creature. ***"And he said unto them, Go ye into all the world, and preach the gospel to every creature. [16] He that believeth and is baptized shall be saved; but he that believeth not shall be damned. [17] And these signs shall follow them***

that believe; In my name shall they cast out devils; they shall speak with new tongues; [18] They shall take up serpents; and if they drink any deadly thing, it shall not hurt them; they shall lay hands on the sick, and they shall recover. [19] So then after the Lord had spoken unto them, he was received up into heaven, and sat on the right hand of God. [20] And they went forth, and preached everywhere, the Lord working with them, and confirming the word with signs following". Amen. *Mark 16:15-20.*

Explaining the vital importance and power inherent in the preaching of the gospel, Apostle Paul said, ***"I am debtor both to the Greeks, and to the Barbarians; both to the wise, and to the unwise. [15] So, as much as in me is, I am ready to preach the gospel to you that are at Rome also. [16] For I am not ashamed of the***

gospel of Christ: for it is the power of God unto salvation to everyone that believeth; to the Jew first, and also to the Greek. [17] For therein is the righteousness of God revealed from faith to faith: as it is written, The just shall live by faith". *Romans 1:14-17.*

The preaching of the gospel ushers in salvation for the believer. Apostle Paul explained the process of salvation in concrete terms in his letter to the church in Rome, when he said, ***"But the righteousness which is of faith speaketh on this wise, Say not in thine heart, Who shall ascend into heaven? (that is, to bring Christ down from above :) [7] Or, Who shall descend into the deep? (that is, to bring up Christ again from the dead.) [8] But what saith it? The word is nigh thee, even in thy mouth, and in thy heart: that is, the word of faith, which we preach; [9]***

That if thou shalt confess with thy mouth the Lord Jesus, and shalt believe in thine heart that God hath raised him from the dead, thou shalt be saved. [10] For with the heart man believeth unto righteousness; and with the mouth confession is made unto salvation. [11] For the scripture saith, Whosoever believeth on him shall not be ashamed. *Romans 10:6-11.*

Describing the various steps that lead to salvation for the believer, Apostle Paul said, ***"For whosoever shall call upon the name of the Lord shall be saved. [14] How then shall they call on him in whom they have not believed? And how shall they believe in him of whom they have not heard? And how shall they hear without a preacher? [15] And how shall they preach, except they be sent? As it is written, How beautiful are the feet of them that preach the***

gospel of peace, and bring glad tidings of good things" *Romans 10:13-15.*

Apostle Paul went further to explain how faith is birthed in the heart of the believer, ***"So then faith cometh by hearing, and hearing by the word of God".*** *Romans 10:17.*

Paul revealed that the effectual communication of the gospel by the power of the Holy Spirit produces faith in the heart of the hearer. ***"But if our gospel be hid, it is hid to them that are lost: [4] In whom the god of this world hath blinded the minds of them which believe not, lest the light of the glorious gospel of Christ, who is the image of God, should shine unto them. [5] For we preach not ourselves, but Christ Jesus the Lord; and ourselves your servants for Jesus' sake. [6] For God, who commanded the light to shine out of darkness,***

hath shined in our hearts, to give the light of the knowledge of the glory of God in the face of Jesus Christ. [7] But we have this treasure in earthen vessels, that the excellency of the power may be of God, and not of us".

2 Corinthians 4:3-7.

As we preach the gospel, Apostle Paul enjoins us to keep our focus on the central theme or message of the gospel, which is the finished works of Christ. Our message must be backed with power as evidence of the gospel of Christ. Without the Holy Spirit, our preaching would be empty and ineffective. Apostle Paul said, ***"And I, brethren, when I came to you, came not with excellency of speech or of wisdom, declaring unto you the testimony of God. [2] For I determined not to know any thing among you, save Jesus Christ, and him crucified. [3] And I***

was with you in weakness, and in fear, and in much trembling. [4] And my speech and my preaching was not with enticing words of man's wisdom, but in demonstration of the Spirit and of power: [5] That your faith should not stand in the wisdom of men, but in the power of God". *1 Corinthians 2:1-5.*

In his letter to the church in Rome, Apostle Paul also said, ***"For I will not dare to speak of any of those things which Christ hath not wrought by me, to make the Gentiles obedient, by word and deed, [19] Through mighty signs and wonders, by the power of the Spirit of God; so that from Jerusalem, and round about unto Illyricum, I have fully preached the gospel of Christ".***
Romans 15:18-19.

He went further to say, ***"For the kingdom of God is not in word, but in power".*** *1 Corinthians 4:20.*

Paul succinctly pointed out the essential ingredients of the gospel in his letter to Timothy, ***"And that from a child thou hast known the holy scriptures, which are able to make thee wise unto salvation through faith which is in Christ Jesus. [16] All scripture is given by inspiration of God, and is profitable for doctrine, for reproof, for correction, for instruction in righteousness: [17] That the man of God may be perfect, throughly furnished unto all good works.*** *2 Timothy 3:15-17.*

The bible admonishes us to be careful with the way or manner in which we receive and handle the gospel of Christ. ***"Therefore we ought to give the more earnest heed to the things which we have heard, lest at any time we should let***

them slip. ***[2] For if the word spoken by angels was stedfast, and every transgression and disobedience received a just recompence of reward; [3] How shall we escape, if we neglect so great salvation; which at the first began to be spoken by the Lord, and was confirmed unto us by them that heard him ; [4] God also bearing them witness, both with signs and wonders, and with divers miracles, and gifts of the Holy Ghost, according to his own will?"*** *Hebrews 2:1-4.*

The bible went further to say, ***"Let us therefore fear, lest, a promise being left us of entering into his rest, any of you should seem to come short of it. [2] For unto us was the gospel preached, as well as unto them: but the word preached did not profit them, not being mixed with faith in them that heard it".*** *Hebrews 4:1-2.*

The Lord Jesus made a profound

statement concerning the word of God. While providing salvation, the same word if rejected will serve as a judge against those that reject him on the Day of Judgment. ***"And if any man hear my words, and believe not, I judge him not: for I came not to judge the world, but to save the world. [48] He that rejecteth me, and receiveth not my words, hath one that judgeth him: the word that I have spoken, the same shall judge him in the last day. [49] For I have not spoken of myself; but the Father which sent me, he gave me a commandment, what I should say, and what I should speak. [50] And I know that his commandment is life everlasting: whatsoever I speak therefore, even as the Father said unto me, so I speak".*** *John 12:47-50.*

In the book of Hebrews, the bible gave a very clear description of the capacity of the Word of God, ***"For the word of God is quick, and powerful, and sharper than any two edged sword, piercing even to the dividing asunder of soul and spirit, and of the joints and marrow, and is a discerner of the thoughts and intents of the heart".*** *Hebrews 4:12.*

As a child of God, the word of God has been committed to your hands. What are you doing with it? What have you done with it? You must make up your mind to put it to work, for yourself, and for your world. Remember, Jesus said, ***"And as ye go, preach, saying, The kingdom of heaven is at hand. [8] Heal the sick, cleanse the lepers, raise the dead, cast out devils: freely ye have received, freely give".***
Matthew 10:7-8.

14

GODLY

The Lord Jesus while on Earth lived a godly life. He practiced and taught his followers to believe in God and the importance of living a Godly and moral life. He was holy, devout, faithful and true in all his dealings. Jesus gave a vivid description of the day of judgment and the criteria for acceptance into heaven when he said, ***"When the Son of man shall come in his glory, and all the holy angels with him, then shall he sit upon the throne of his glory: [32] And before him shall be gathered all nations: and he shall separate them one from another, as a shepherd divideth his sheep from the goats: [33] And he***

shall set the sheep on his right hand, but the goats on the left. [34] Then shall the King say unto them on his right hand, Come, ye blessed of my Father, inherit the kingdom prepared for you from the foundation of the world: [35] For I was an hungred, and ye gave me meat: I was thirsty, and ye gave me drink: I was a stranger, and ye took me in: [36] Naked, and ye clothed me: I was sick, and ye visited me: I was in prison, and ye came unto me. [37] Then shall the righteous answer him, saying, Lord, when saw we thee an hungred, and fed thee? or thirsty, and gave thee drink? [38] When saw we thee a stranger, and took thee in? or naked, and clothed thee? [39] Or when saw we thee sick, or in prison, and came unto thee? [40] And the King shall answer and say unto them, Verily I say unto you, Inasmuch as ye have done it unto

one of the least of these my brethren, ye have done it unto me. [41] Then shall he say also unto them on the left hand, Depart from me, ye cursed, into everlasting fire, prepared for the devil and his angels: [42] For I was an hungred, and ye gave me no meat: I was thirsty, and ye gave me no drink: [43] I was a stranger, and ye took me not in: naked, and ye clothed me not: sick, and in prison, and ye visited me not. [44] Then shall they also answer him, saying, Lord, when saw we thee an hungred, or athirst, or a stranger, or naked, or sick, or in prison, and did not minister unto thee? [45] Then shall he answer them, saying, Verily I say unto you, Inasmuch as ye did it not to one of the least of these, ye did it not to me. [46] And these shall go away into everlasting punishment: but the righteous into life eternal". *Matthew 25:31-46.*

In one of his sermons, Jesus outlined the standards for godly living when he said, ***"But I say unto you which hear, Love your enemies, do good to them which hate you, [28] Bless them that curse you, and pray for them which despitefully use you. [29] And unto him that smiteth thee on the one cheek offer also the other; and him that taketh away thy cloke forbid not to take thy coat also. [30] Give to every man that asketh of thee; and of him that taketh away thy goods ask them not again. [31] And as ye would that men should do to you, do ye also to them likewise. [32] For if ye love them which love you, what thank have ye? for sinners also love those that love them. [33] And if ye do good to them which do good to you, what thank have ye? for sinners also do even the same. [34] And if ye lend to them of whom ye hope to receive, what***

thank have ye? for sinners also lend to sinners, to receive as much again". *Luke 6:27-34.*

Driving his message deeper and clearer, the Lord said to the people, ***"But love ye your enemies, and do good, and lend, hoping for nothing again; and your reward shall be great, and ye shall be the children of the Highest: for he is kind unto the unthankful and to the evil. [36] Be ye therefore merciful, as your Father also is merciful. [37] Judge not, and ye shall not be judged: condemn not, and ye shall not be condemned: forgive, and ye shall be forgiven: [38] Give, and it shall be given unto you; good measure, pressed down, and shaken together, and running over, shall men give into your bosom. For with the same measure that ye mete withal it shall be measured to you again".***

Luke 6:35-38.

The Lord reminds us through the scripture above that a godly man must: love his enemies, do good to those that hate him, bless them that curse him, pray for them that treat him despitefully; never strike back when struck, must not resist those that take away their goods, lend to borrowers without expecting anything in return; must be merciful, must not judge others, must not condemn others, must always forgive, must give liberally to the poor, the needy and to others. In the gospel of Matthew, the Lord listed some of the attributes of a godly person, ***"And he opened his mouth, and taught them, saying, [3] Blessed are the poor in spirit: for theirs is the kingdom of heaven. [4] Blessed are they that mourn: for they shall be comforted. [5] Blessed are the meek: for they shall inherit the earth. [6] Blessed are they which do hunger and thirst***

after righteousness: for they shall be filled. [7] Blessed are the merciful: for they shall obtain mercy. [8] Blessed are the pure in heart: for they shall see God. [9] Blessed are the peacemakers: for they shall be called the children of God. [10] Blessed are they which are persecuted for righteousness' sake: for theirs is the kingdom of heaven. [11] Blessed are ye, when men shall revile you, and persecute you, and shall say all manner of evil against you falsely, for my sake. [12] Rejoice, and be exceeding glad: for great is your reward in heaven: for so persecuted they the prophets which were before you".

Matthew 5:2-12.

Apostle Paul addressed some pertinent issues in his letter to the various churches. These issues bother on godly living, especially with new members who were not Jews and were not living under the Mosaic Law. The new converts were saddled with the conflict of their former ways of life and the new godly living required as followers of Christ. In his letter to the church at Ephesus, Apostle Paul wrote, ***"This I say therefore, and testify in the Lord, that ye henceforth walk not as other Gentiles walk, in the vanity of their mind, [18] Having the understanding darkened, being alienated from the life of God through the ignorance that is in them, because of the blindness of their heart: [19] Who being past feeling have given themselves over unto lasciviousness, to work all uncleanness with greediness. [20] But ye have not so learned Christ; [21] If so be that ye have heard him, and have been taught by him, as the truth is in Jesus: [22] That ye put off concerning the former conversation the old man, which is***

corrupt according to the deceitful lusts; [23] And be renewed in the spirit of your mind; [24] And that ye put on the new man, which after God is created in righteousness and true holiness". *Ephesians 4:17-24.*

Apostle Paul went further to provide them with some instructions to guide them in their daily living as people of God. ***"Wherefore putting away lying, speak every man truth with his neighbour: for we are members one of another. [26] Be ye angry, and sin not: let not the sun go down upon your wrath: [27] Neither give place to the devil. [28] Let him that stole steal no more: but rather let him labour, working with his hands the thing which is good, that he may have to give to him that needeth. [29] Let no corrupt communication proceed out of your mouth, but that which is good to the use of***

edifying, that it may minister grace unto the hearers. [30] And grieve not the Holy Spirit of God, whereby ye are sealed unto the day of redemption. [31] Let all bitterness, and wrath, and anger, and clamour, and evil speaking, be put away from you, with all malice: [32] And be ye kind one to another, tenderhearted, forgiving one another, even as God for Christ's sake hath forgiven you". *Ephesians 4:25-32.*

Another serious problem was addressed by Apostle Paul in the Church at Corinth. There were issues of members taking other believers to court. There were also issues of fraud among members resulting in court cases. Apostle Paul condemned such behaviors in very strong terms. ***"Dare any of you, having a matter against another, go to law before the unjust, and not before the saints? [2] Do ye not know that the***

saints shall judge the world? And if the world shall be judged by you, are ye unworthy to judge the smallest matters? [3] Know ye not that we shall judge angels? How much more things that pertain to this life? [4] If then ye have judgments of things pertaining to this life, set them to judge who are least esteemed in the church. [5] I speak to your shame. Is it so, that there is not a wise man among you? No, not one that shall be able to judge between his brethren? [6] But brother goeth to law with brother and that before the unbelievers. [7] Now therefore there is utterly a fault among you, because ye go to law one with another. Why do ye not rather take wrong? Why do ye not rather suffer yourselves to be defrauded? [8] Nay, ye do wrong, and defraud, and that your brethren".

1 Corinthians 6:1-8.

15

THE LIVING AND ACTIVE WORD

Before his birth on Earth, the Word of God was received by Moses as the laws of God and by the prophets under the inspiration of the Holy Spirit. The children of Israel found it practically impossible to obey the laws of God given by Moses. Despite the warnings by the prophets, the people of Israel could not help but disobey God. The righteous laws given by God to bring his people close to him only served to judge them. Jesus came as the incarnate of God's Word. He is the Word of God in human form. This was aptly described by the Apostle John in his gospel when he said, ***"And the Word was made flesh, and***

dwelt among us, (and we beheld his glory, the glory as of the only begotten of the Father,) full of grace and truth". *John 1:14.*

In his letter to the church in Rome, Paul made reference to the same truth, ***"Paul, a servant of Jesus Christ, called to be an apostle, separated unto the gospel of God, [2] (Which he had promised afore by his prophets in the holy scriptures,) [3] Concerning his Son Jesus Christ our Lord, which was made of the seed of David according to the flesh; [4] And declared to be the Son of God with power, according to the spirit of holiness, by the resurrection from the dead".*** *Romans 1:1-4.*

Apostle Paul made the same assertion in his letter to the Philippians Church when he said concerning Jesus, ***"Let this mind be in you, which was also in Christ Jesus: [6] Who, being***

in the form of God, thought it not robbery to be equal with God: [7] But made himself of no reputation, and took upon him the form of a servant, and was made in the likeness of men". *Philippians 2:5-7.*

Making reference to the challenges associated with the law, Apostle Paul said, ***"For the law of the Spirit of life in Christ Jesus hath made me free from the law of sin and death. [3] For what the law could not do, in that it was weak through the flesh, God sending his own Son in the likeness of sinful flesh, and for sin, condemned sin in the flesh".*** *Romans 8:2-3.*

Clarifying the divinity of the man Jesus, Apostle Paul wrote to Timothy saying, ***"And without controversy great is the mystery of godliness: God was manifest in the flesh, justified in the Spirit, seen of angels, preached***

unto the Gentiles, believed on in the world, received up into glory". *1 Timothy 3:16.*

In the book of Hebrews, the bible said concerning the incarnation of Jesus, ***"Forasmuch then as the children are partakers of flesh and blood, he also himself likewise took part of the same; that through death he might destroy him that had the power of death, that is, the devil; [15] And deliver them who through fear of death were all their lifetime subject to bondage".*** *Hebrews 2:14-15.*

When we received Jesus as our Lord and savior, we received his nature and the power to become sons of God, and thus Word of God. Apostle Peter gave a vivid description of this new birth when he said, ***"Being born again, not of corruptible seed, but of incorruptible, by the***

word of God, which liveth and abideth for ever". *1 Peter 1:23.*

Apostle John wrote about the believer's new birth and root in God when he said, ***"But as many as received him, to them gave he power to become the sons of God, even to them that believe on his name: [13] Which were born, not of blood, nor of the will of the flesh, nor of the will of man, but of God".*** *John 1:12-13.*

In his letter to the Galatians church, Apostle Paul confirmed our new status as sons of God and joint heirs with Jesus, ***"But when the fullness of the time was come, God sent forth his Son, made of a woman, made under the law, [5] To redeem them that were under the law, that we might receive the adoption of sons. [6] And because ye are sons, God hath sent forth the Spirit of his Son into your hearts, crying, Abba,***

Father. [7] Wherefore thou art no more a servant, but a son; and if a son, then an heir of God through Christ. *Galatians 4:4-7.*

When we received Christ, we became children of God. As children of God, we are born of the Word of God. We live and draw our nourishment from the word of God. God expects us to live as his living Word on Earth. Just as Jesus, we are born of the Word. Everything about us should reflect the living and active Word of God. We are the Word of God in motion, doing the will and pleasure of God on the Earth. Apostle Paul gave a very beautiful description of how we should live and draw our inspiration from the Word. Paul referred to the Word of God as the mirror of God. He said that as we continue to look into the mirror of God (Word of God), we are being transformed into the same image, from one level of glory to another. ***"But we all, with open face beholding as in a glass the glory of the Lord, are changed into the same image from glory to glory, even as by the Spirit of the Lord".*** *2 Corinthians 3:18.*

From the above scripture, we realize that the Word of God is the mirror of God. As we look into the mirror of God (Word of God), we see ourselves: who we are and what God has said concerning us and has planned for us. As we continue to look into the mirror of God, we are being transformed into the same image, from one level of glory to another, into ever increasing glory, by the Spirit of the Lord. The Apostle James confirmed this in his epistle when he said, ***"But be ye doers of the word, and not hearers only, deceiving your own selves. [23] For if any be a hearer of the word, and not a doer, he is like***

unto a man beholding his natural face in a glass: [24] For he beholdeth himself, and goeth his way, and straightway forgetteth what manner of man he was. [25] But whoso looketh into the perfect law of liberty, and continueth therein, he being not a forgetful hearer, but a doer of the work, this man shall be blessed in his deed". *James 1:22-25.*

In the gospel of Luke, the bible recorded a profound parable made by Jesus during one of his teachings about the effectiveness of the Word of God in the lives of the people (the hearers). ***"And when much people were gathered together, and were come to him out of every city, he spake by a parable: [5] A sower went out to sow his seed: and as he sowed, some fell by the way side; and it was trodden down, and the fowls of the air devoured it. [6] And some fell upon a rock; and***

as soon as it was sprung up, it withered away, because it lacked moisture. [7] And some fell among thorns; and the thorns sprang up with it, and choked it. [8] And other fell on good ground, and sprang up, and bare fruit an hundredfold. And when he had said these things, he cried, He that hath ears to hear, let him hear. [9] And his disciples asked him, saying, What might this parable be? [10] And he said, Unto you it is given to know the mysteries of the kingdom of God: but to others in parables; that seeing they might not see, and hearing they might not understand. [11] Now the parable is this: The seed is the word of God. [12] Those by the way side are they that hear; then cometh the devil, and taketh away the word out of their hearts, lest they should believe and be saved. [13] They on the rock are they, which, when they hear, receive

the word with joy; and these have no root, which for a while believe, and in time of temptation fall away. [14] And that which fell among thorns are they, which, when they have heard, go forth, and are choked with cares and riches and pleasures of this life, and bring no fruit to perfection. [15] But that on the good ground are they, which in an honest and good heart, having heard the word, keep it, and bring forth fruit with patience". *Luke 8:4-15.*

From the Lord's teaching highlighted in the scripture above we can deduce that the effectiveness of God's Word in the life of a man is determined by the condition of his heart. The things that attack the Word when received, making it ineffective are: the devil, which comes to take the Word from the heart of men, lest they should believe and be saved. Jesus said the seed that fell by the wayside were taken away by the devil. The wayside is the foot path on which men walk by. When we allow our heart to be ruled or influenced by the ideas and suggestions of men, this gives room for the devil to come in and take away the Word of God from our hearts. We must subject ourselves under the lordship of God's word and not the opinions and suggestions from news, social media, peer groups and family affiliations. To deal with this issue, we must accept Jesus as Lord and subject ourselves under the authority of God's Word. This makes us children of God and heirs of salvation. The new birth puts us in a position to receive from God without hindrance from the devil.

The second issue outlined in the Lord's teaching is temptation. The challenge of temptation is dealt with by sufficient exposure to and study of God's word. The more of God's Word we receive, the greater is our faith built up. As we build our faith strong through the increased exposure to the Word of God, we are able to withstand the devil and overcome temptation and tribulation. The third issue that frustrates the effectiveness of God's word in our lives is the cares, and riches and pleasures of this life. The Lord clearly stated that cares, and riches, and pleasures of this life are like thorns which choke the Word of God in the heart of men, making the Word of God ineffective. We are required to give our hearts wholly to the Lord and depend on him to meet our needs according to his riches in glory by Christ Jesus. Until we are willing to give the Lord our attention and look away from distractions; we may never be able to produce fruits. The Lord concluded by saying that the heart that produced good fruit is the honest and good heart that received the Word with patience. Jesus is the living and active Word of God. As sons of God, we are the living Word also. God expects us to live as his active Word in our worlds

16

EXEMPLARY LIFESTYLE – THE LIGHT

The Lord Jesus lived an exemplary life on Earth, and set a perfect example for the children of God. His life was so perfect that the Sanhedrin (the Jewish leaders) could not find any reason to accuse him before the Roman authorities. When he was brought before the Roman authorities, they saw no grounds to sentence him. Jesus lived a blameless life before God and man. The bible recorded in the book of Hebrews, ***"For we have not an high priest which cannot be touched with the feeling of our infirmities; but was in all points tempted like as we are, yet without sin"*** . *Hebrews 4:15.*

Apostle Paul in his letter to the church in Corinth, pointed to the sinless nature of Jesus when he said, ***"For he hath made him to be sin for us, who knew no sin; that we might be made the righteousness of God in him".*** *2 Corinthians 5:21.*

The bible further declares concerning Jesus, ***"For such an high priest became us, who is holy, harmless, undefiled, separate from sinners, and made higher than the heavens".*** *Hebrews 7:26.*

The prophet Isaiah spoke concerning the coming Messiah and his ministry. In his prophecy, he emphasized his sinless nature when he said, ***"Surely he hath borne our griefs, and carried our sorrows: yet we did esteem him stricken, smitten of God, and afflicted. [5] But he was wounded for our transgressions; he was***

bruised for our iniquities: the chastisement of our peace was upon him; and with his stripes we are healed. [6] All we like sheep have gone astray; we have turned every one to his own way; and the Lord hath laid on him the iniquity of us all. [7] He was oppressed, and he was afflicted, yet he opened not his mouth: he is brought as a lamb to the slaughter, and as a sheep before her shearers is dumb, so he openeth not his mouth. [8] He was taken from prison and from judgment: and who shall declare his generation? For he was cut off out of the land of the living: for the transgression of my people was he stricken. [9] And he made his grave with the wicked and with the rich in his death; because he had done no violence, neither was any deceit in his mouth".

Isaiah 53:4-9.

Apostle Peter, in his epistle to the churches affirmed this same position when he said, ***"For even hereunto were ye called: because Christ also suffered for us, leaving us an example, that ye should follow his steps: [22] Who did no sin, neither was guile found in his mouth: [23] Who, when he was reviled, reviled not again; when he suffered, he threatened not; but committed himself to him that judgeth righteously".*** *1 Peter 2:21-23.*

In his first epistle to the churches, Apostle John confirmed the same truth when he said, ***"And ye know that he was manifested to take away our sins; and in him is no sin".***

1 John 3:5.

Describing himself during his days on Earth, Jesus said, ***"As long as I am in the world, I am the light of the world".*** *John 9:5.*

That is a very profound statement because light is that which defines, which informs, and which enlightens. Light establishes the basis for reference, appraisal and confirmation. The Lord Jesus as the light becomes the basis for our reference or our point of reference. Distinguishing himself from the world, the Lord said, ***"I am come a light into the world, that whosoever believeth on me should not abide in darkness"****. John 12:46.*

Emphasizing his vital role in the lives of his followers, he said, ***"Then spake Jesus again unto them, saying, I am the light of the world: he that followeth me shall not walk in darkness, but shall have the light of life"*** *John 8:12.*

In the book of Proverbs, the bible declares, ***"The spirit of man is the candle of the***

Lord, searching all the inward parts of the belly". *Proverbs 20:27.*

The bible refers to the spirit of man as the candle of the Lord. Unfortunately, man's candle is unlit and therefore man has been in darkness until the coming of Christ. Man has been under the control of the powers of darkness (domain of darkness) and helpless until Jesus came. Apostle John aptly described the essence of Christ when he said, ***"In him was life; and the life was the light of men. [5] And the light shineth in darkness; and the darkness comprehended it not".*** *John 1:4-5.*

Connecting the ministry of Christ and the spirit of man which was in darkness, Apostle John declared, "***That was the true Light, which lighteth every man that cometh into the world".*** *John 1:9.*

Jesus came to lighten the spirit of man making them effective (lit) candles in the hands of the Lord. The Lord expressly stated this fact when he said, ***"I am come a light into the world, that whosoever believeth on me should not abide in darkness".*** *John 12:46.*

However, the power to choose given by God to man determines man's fate. The Lord revealed the basis for his appraisal when he said, ***"For God sent not his Son into the world to condemn the world; but that the world through him might be saved. [18] He that believeth on him is not condemned: but he that believeth not is condemned already, because he hath not believed in the name of the only begotten Son of God. [19] And this is the condemnation, that light is come into the world, and men loved***

darkness rather than light, because their deeds were evil". *John 3:17-19.*

Jesus came to lighten us and make us children of light. As children of light, we have been made lights to our worlds. Jesus revealed this truth when he said, ***"While ye have light, believe in the light, that ye may be the children of light..."*** *John 12:36.*

Emphasizing our new roles and duties as products of light, the lord said, ***"Ye are the light of the world. A city that is set on an hill cannot be hid. [15] Neither do men light a candle, and put it under a bushel, but on a candlestick; and it giveth light unto all that are in the house. [16] Let your light so shine before men, that they may see your good works, and glorify your Father which is in heaven.***

Matthew 5:14-16

In his letter to the Philippians church Apostle Paul encouraged the believers to live as lights in their world. ***"Do all things without murmurings and disputings: [15] That ye may be blameless and harmless, the sons of God, without rebuke, in the midst of a crooked and perverse nation, among whom ye shine as lights in the world"*** *Philippians 2:14-15.*

Jesus lived an exemplary life and expects us as children of God to do same. He set the standard for us to live by. Apostle Peter, in his first epistle to the churches said something beautiful regarding our status as sons of light, ***"But ye are a chosen generation, a royal priesthood, an holy nation, a peculiar people; that ye should shew forth the praises of him who hath called you out of darkness into his marvellous light"***

1 Peter 2:9.

We are called to be lights to our world. Apostle Paul in his letter to the church in Rome described the duty of children of God, to serve as role models and points of reference to their world when he said. ***"For the earnest expectation of the creature waiteth for the manifestation of the sons of God. [20] For the creature was made subject to vanity, not willingly, but by reason of him who hath subjected the same in hope, [21] Because the creature itself also shall be delivered from the bondage of corruption into the glorious liberty of the children of God.*** *Romans 8:19-21.*

Apostle Paul from the above scripture revealed that the whole of creation and (or) creature is waiting for the manifestation of the sons of God. This is because the creatures are subject to, and under the control of the powers of darkness. Unless and until the sons of light take their proper place and assume authority and control over all of God's creation, the creatures will remain in bondage. The sons of light are required to grow into maturity and assume the duty of liberating the creatures and allowing them to enjoy the liberty of the children of God. For example, money in the hands of the unbeliever is mostly used for evil. Money in the hands of the unbeliever cries out asking to be liberated from the hands of the unbeliever, and be used for the glory of God.

17

GODLIKE

The Lord Jesus manifested the nature of God while on Earth. He revealed the thoughts and intents of God behind the laws given to Moses for the people of God. Jesus provided a pristine insight into the laws of God. Who would have believed that our offerings are not acceptable to God when we have grievances with others? Jesus said, ***"Therefore if thou bring thy gift to the altar, and there rememberest that thy brother hath ought against thee; [24] Leave there thy gift before the altar, and go thy way; first be reconciled to thy brother, and then come and offer thy gift".*** *Matthew 5:23-24.*

On the strict observance of the Sabbath , Jesus demonstrated that God is more pleased with doing good works on the Sabbath than observing the rest associatd with the Sabbath. Jesus consistently ministered healing to the sick on the Sabbath and taught the people that accommodating evil or showing of piety without sincerity on the Sabbath is displeasing to God. He condemned the religious leaders who would force the people to strictly observe the Sabbath while they secretly do otherwise. ***"And he was teaching in one of the synagogues on the Sabbath. [11] And, behold, there was a woman which had a spirit of infirmity eighteen years, and was bowed together, and could in no wise lift up herself. [12] And when Jesus saw her, he called her to him, and said unto her, Woman, thou art loosed from thine*** infirmity.

[13] And he laid his hands on her: and immediately she was made straight, and glorified God. [14] And the ruler of the synagogue answered with indignation, because that Jesus had healed on the Sabbath day, and said unto the people, There are six days in which men ought to work: in them therefore come and be healed, and not on the Sabbath day. [15] The Lord then answered him, and said, Thou hypocrite, doth not each one of you on the Sabbath loose his ox or his ass from the stall, and lead him away to watering? [16] And ought not this woman, being a daughter of Abraham, whom Satan hath bound, lo, these eighteen years, be loosed from this bond on the Sabbath day? [17] And when he had said these things, all his adversaries were ashamed: and all the people rejoiced for all the glorious things that

were done by him". *Luke 13:10-17.*

Jesus taught the people how God expects them to handle offences. ***"Ye have heard that it hath been said, An eye for an eye, and a tooth for a tooth: [39] But I say unto you, That ye resist not evil: but whosoever shall smite thee on thy right cheek, turn to him the other also. [40] And if any man will sue thee at the law, and take away thy coat, let him have thy cloke also. [41] And whosoever shall compel thee to go a mile, go with him twain. [42] Give to him that asketh thee, and from him that would borrow of thee turn not thou away. [43] Ye have heard that it hath been said, Thou shalt love thy neighbour, and hate thine enemy. [44] But I say unto you, Love your enemies, bless them that curse you, do good to them that hate you, and pray for them which despitefully use you, and persecute you;***

[45] That ye may be the children of your Father which is in heaven: for he maketh his sun to rise on the evil and on the good, and sendeth rain on the just and on the unjust". *Matthew 5:38-45.*

On issues of honesty and sincerity, the Lord expects his people to exhibit the highest level of integrity and honesty. Their word must simply be 'Yes' or 'No'. ***"Again, ye have heard that it hath been said by them of old time, Thou shalt not forswear thyself, but shalt perform unto the Lord thine oaths: [34] But I say unto you, Swear not at all; neither by heaven; for it is God's throne: [35] Nor by the earth; for it is his footstool: neither by Jerusalem; for it is the city of the great King. [36] Neither shalt thou swear by thy head, because thou canst not make one hair white or black. [37] But let your communication be, Yea, yea; Nay, nay: for***

whatsoever is more than these cometh of evil". *Matthew 5:33-37.*

The Lord clearly explained how God values and appreciates our word. Like him, God expects us to understand the potency of our words and the consequence of using them wrongly. Furthermore, the Lord expects us to keep our words when we make commitments to him or to others. He frowns at anyone who is unwilling to keep his word or commitment. Jesus said something very interesting on the issue of murder or killing. While we appreciate the gravity of taking someone's life, the Lord revealed the deeper intent of God when he said we must not kill, and what he considers as murder. ***"Ye have heard that it was said by them of old time, Thou shalt not kill; and whosoever shall kill shall be in danger of the judgment: [22] But I say unto***

you, That whosoever is angry with his brother without a cause shall be in danger of the judgment: and whosoever shall say to his brother, Raca, shall be in danger of the council: but whosoever shall say, Thou fool, shall be in danger of hell fire". *Matthew 5:21-22.*

This brings to mind the question Peter asked Jesus concerning the number of times he must forgive his brother when he offends him. ***"Then came Peter to him, and said, Lord, how oft shall my brother sin against me, and I forgive him? Till seven times? [22] Jesus saith unto him, I say not unto thee, Until seven times: but, Until seventy times seven".*** *Matthew 18:21-22.*

The Lord went further to illustrate this teaching with a parable to show the mind of God and his expectations from us regarding forgiveness. ***"Therefore is the kingdom of***

heaven likened unto a certain king, which would take account of his servants. [24] And when he had begun to reckon, one was brought unto him, which owed him ten thousand talents. [25] But forasmuch as he had not to pay, his lord commanded him to be sold, and his wife, and children, and all that he had, and payment to be made. [26] The servant therefore fell down, and worshipped him, saying, Lord, have patience with me, and I will pay thee all. [27] Then the lord of that servant was moved with compassion, and loosed him, and forgave him the debt. [28] But the same servant went out, and found one of his fellow servants, which owed him an hundred pence: and he laid hands on him, and took him by the throat, saying, Pay me that thou owest. [29] And his fellow servant fell down at his feet, and besought him, saying, Have patience with

me, and I will pay thee all. [30] And he would not: but went and cast him into prison, till he should pay the debt. [31] So when his fellow servants saw what was done, they were very sorry, and came and told unto their lord all that was done. [32] Then his lord, after that he had called him, said unto him, O thou wicked servant, I forgave thee all that debt, because thou desiredst me: [33] Shouldest not thou also have had compassion on thy fellow servant, even as I had pity on thee? [34] And his lord was wroth, and delivered him to the tormentors, till he should pay all that was due unto him. [35] So likewise shall my heavenly Father do also unto you, if ye from your hearts forgive not everyone his brother their trespasses".

Matthew 18:23-35.

On the issue of adultery, the Lord said something very profound, ***"Ye have heard that it was said by them of old time, Thou shalt not commit adultery: [28] But I say unto you, That whosoever looketh on a woman to lust after her hath committed adultery with her already in his heart".*** *Matthew 5:27-28.*

The lord revealed that God judges the intents of the heart as well as the actions. Our hearts must always be right before God. The Lord expects our spirits to gain ascendency over our thoughts and emotions. The bible declares, ***"For they that are after the flesh do mind the things of the flesh; but they that are after the Spirit the things of the Spirit. [6] For to be carnally minded is death; but to be spiritually minded is life and peace. [7] Because the carnal mind is enmity against God: for it is not subject to the***

law of God, neither indeed can be. [8] So then they that are in the flesh cannot please God". *Romans 8:5-8.*

A carnal man is one that is ruled by his senses. But the spiritual man is one that is yielded to the Spirit of God. On the subject of divorce, the Lord condemned the act in very concrete terms. ***"And the Pharisees came to him, and asked him, Is it lawful for a man to put away his wife? Tempting him. [3] And he answered and said unto them, What did Moses command you? [4] And they said, Moses suffered to write a bill of divorcement, and to put her away. [5] And Jesus answered and said unto them, For the hardness of your heart he wrote you this precept. [6] But from the beginning of the creation God made them male and female. [7] For this cause shall a man leave his father and mother, and cleave to***

his wife; [8] And they twain shall be one flesh: so then they are no more twain, but one flesh. [9] What therefore God hath joined together, let not man put asunder". *Mark 10:2-9.*

Clarifying this teaching to his disciples privately, ***"And he saith unto them, Whosoever shall put away his wife, and marry another, committeth adultery against her. [12] And if a woman shall put away her husband, and be married to another, she committeth adultery".*** *Mark 10:11-12.*

On the subject of charitable giving, Jesus revealed the proper manner we should do our charitable giving for it to be acceptable to God, ***"Take heed that ye do not your alms before men, to be seen of them: otherwise ye have no reward of your Father which is in heaven. [2] Therefore when thou doest thine alms, do not sound a***

trumpet before thee, as the hypocrites do in the synagogues and in the streets, that they may have glory of men. Verily I say unto you, They have their reward. [3] But when thou doest alms, let not thy left hand know what thy right hand doeth: [4] That thine alms may be in secret: and thy Father which seeth in secret himself shall reward thee openly". *Matthew 6:1-4.*

On the subject of fasting, the Lord explained how we must carry out our fasting to make it effective and acceptable to God. ***"Moreover when ye fast, be not, as the hypocrites, of a sad countenance: for they disfigure their faces, that they may appear unto men to fast. Verily I say unto you, They have their reward. [17] But thou, when thou fastest, anoint thine head, and wash thy face; [18] That thou appear not unto men to fast, but unto thy***

Father which is in secret: and thy Father, which seeth in secret, shall reward thee openly". *Matthew 6:16-18.*

The Lord gave a remarkable teaching on how to pray effectively and receive results. ***"And when thou prayest, thou shalt not be as the hypocrites are: for they love to pray standing in the synagogues and in the corners of the streets, that they may be seen of men. Verily I say unto you, They have their reward. [6] But thou, when thou prayest, enter into thy closet, and when thou hast shut thy door, pray to thy Father which is in secret; and thy Father which seeth in secret shall reward thee openly. [7] But when ye pray, use not vain repetitions, as the heathen do: for they think that they shall be heard for their much speaking. [8] Be not ye therefore like unto them: for your Father knoweth what things ye***

have need of, before ye ask him". *Matthew 6:5-8.*

Jesus dealt with the issue of leadership in a very significant way. He instructed that leaders should be servants and not masters. The position of leadership according to him is that of service and not lordship. ***"And there was also a strife among them, which of them should be accounted the greatest. [25] And he said unto them, The kings of the Gentiles exercise lordship over them; and they that exercise authority upon them are called benefactors. [26] But ye shall not be so: but he that is greatest among you let him be as the younger; and he that is chief, as he that doth serve".***
Luke 22:24-26.

Apostle Mark in his gospel recorded a more detailed account of this incident and the response of Jesus. ***"And James and John, the***

sons of Zebedee, come unto him, saying, Master, we would that thou shouldest do for us whatsoever we shall desire. [36] And he said unto them, What would ye that I should do for you? [37] They said unto him, Grant unto us that we may sit, one on thy right hand, and the other on thy left hand, in thy glory. [38] But Jesus said unto them, Ye know not what ye ask: can ye drink of the cup that I drink of? And be baptized with the baptism that I am baptized with? [39] And they said unto him, We can. And Jesus said unto them, Ye shall indeed drink of the cup that I drink of; and with the baptism that I am baptized withal shall ye be baptized: [40] But to sit on my right hand and on my left hand is not mine to give; but it shall be given to them for whom it is prepared. [41] And when the ten heard it, they began to be much displeased with

James and John. [42] But Jesus called them to him, and saith unto them, Ye know that they which are accounted to rule over the Gentiles exercise lordship over them; and their great ones exercise authority upon them. [43] But so shall it not be among you: but whosoever will be great among you, shall be your minister: [44] And whosoever of you will be the chiefest, shall be servant of all. [45] For even the Son of man came not to be ministered unto, but to minister and to give his life a ransom for many".

Mark 10:35-45.

On a certain day Jesus had an encounter with a rich young ruler. During the conversation, the lord revealed the challenges associated with placing one's confidence on wealth and riches. Having confidence in riches comes at the risk of one's salvation. ***"And when he was gone forth*** *into the way, there came one running, and kneeled to him, and asked him, Good Master, what shall I do that I may inherit eternal life? [18] And Jesus said unto him, Why callest thou me good? There is none good but one, that is, God. [19] Thou knowest the commandments, Do not commit adultery, Do not kill, Do not steal, Do not bear false witness, Defraud not, Honour thy father and mother. [20] And he answered and said unto him, Master, all these have I observed from my youth. [21] Then Jesus beholding him loved him, and said unto him, One thing thou lackest: go thy way, sell whatsoever thou hast, and give to the poor, and thou shalt have treasure in heaven: and come, take up the cross, and follow me. [22] And he was sad at that saying, and went away grieved: for he had great possessions. [23] And Jesus*

looked round about, and saith unto his disciples, How hardly shall they that have riches enter into the kingdom of God! [24] And the disciples were astonished at his words. But Jesus answereth again, and saith unto them, Children, how hard is it for them that trust in riches to enter into the kingdom of God! [25] It is easier for a camel to go through the eye of a needle, than for a rich man to enter into the kingdom of God".

Mark 10:17-25.

This point was emphasized by the Lord when he said, ***"No man can serve two masters: for either he will hate the one, and love the other; or else he will hold to the one, and despise the other. Ye cannot serve God and mammon".***

Matthew 6:24.

When the Lord taught his disciples on the effectiveness of the Word in the lives of the believers, he outlined the deceitfulness of riches as one of the major challenges to the effectiveness of God's Word in the lives of the children of God. Trust in riches causes God's word to be unfruitful in the lives of his people. ***"He also that received seed among the thorns is he that heareth the word; and the care of this world, and the deceitfulness of riches, choke the word, and he becometh unfruitful".*** *Matthew 13:22.*

The Lord Jesus gave a parable concerning the foolishness of placing one's hope on earthly riches and wealth. ***"And he spake a parable unto them, saying, The ground of a certain rich man brought forth plentifully: [17] And he thought within himself, saying, What shall I do, because I have no room where to bestow my fruits? [18] And he said, This will I do: I will pull down my barns, and build greater;***

and there will I bestow all my fruits and my goods. [19] And I will say to my soul, Soul, thou hast much goods laid up for many years; take thine ease, eat, drink, and be merry. [20] But God said unto him, Thou fool, this night thy soul shall be required of thee: then whose shall those things be, which thou hast provided? [21] So is he that layeth up treasure for himself, and is not rich toward God". *Luke 12:16-21.*

The Lord offered a counsel on what better to do than to trust in riches, ***"Sell that ye have, and give alms; provide yourselves bags which wax not old, a treasure in the heavens that faileth not, where no thief approacheth, neither moth corrupteth. [34] For where your treasure is, there will your heart be also".***

Luke 12:33-34

Amplifying this point, Apostle Paul in his

letter to Timothy said, ***"But they that will be rich fall into temptation and a snare, and into many foolish and hurtful lusts, which drown men in destruction and perdition. [10] For the love of money is the root of all evil: which while some coveted after, they have erred from the faith, and pierced themselves through with many sorrows".*** *1 Timothy 6:9-10.*

Addressing the issue of anxiety and worries concerning the needs of life, Jesus made a sensitive pronouncement, ***"Therefore I say unto you, Take no thought for your life, what ye shall eat, or what ye shall drink; nor yet for your body, what ye shall put on. Is not the life more than meat, and the body than raiment? [26] Behold the fowls of the air: for they sow not, neither do they reap, nor gather into barns; yet your heavenly Father feedeth them. Are ye not much***

better than they? [27] Which of you by taking thought can add one cubit unto his stature? [28] And why take ye thought for raiment? Consider the lilies of the field, how they grow; they toil not, neither do they spin: [29] And yet I say unto you, That even Solomon in all his glory was not arrayed like one of these. [30] Wherefore, if God so clothe the grass of the field, which to day is, and to morrow is cast into the oven, shall he not much more clothe you, O ye of little faith? [31] Therefore take no thought, saying, What shall we eat? or, What shall we drink? or, Wherewithal shall we be clothed? [32] (For after all these things do the Gentiles seek) for your heavenly Father knoweth that ye have need of all these things". *Matthew 6:25-32.*

He concluded this teaching by saying, ***"Take therefore no thought for the morrow: for***

the morrow shall take thought for the things of itself. Sufficient unto the day is the evil thereof" *Matthew 6:34.*

Apostle Paul confirmed this teaching in his letter to the Philippians church when he said, ***"Be careful for nothing; but in every thing by prayer and supplication with thanksgiving let your requests be made known unto God. [7] And the peace of God, which passeth all understanding, shall keep your hearts and minds through Christ Jesus".*** *Philippians 4:6-7.*

Apostle Peter echoed same teaching in his epistle when he said, ***"Casting all your care upon him; for he careth for you".*** *1 Peter 5:7.*

The Lord Jesus spelt out man's number one priority in life. This priority ranks first in God's order of importance. Jesus said, ***"But seek ye first the kingdom of God, and his***

righteousness; and all these things shall be added unto you". *Matthew 6:33.*

When Peter engaged Jesus in a conversation concerning their reward for leaving all to follow him, Jesus made a remarkable statement, ***"Then Peter began to say unto him, Lo, we have left all, and have followed thee. [29] And Jesus answered and said, Verily I say unto you, There is no man that hath left house, or brethren, or sisters, or father, or mother, or wife, or children, or lands, for my sake, and the gospel's, [30] But he shall receive an hundredfold now in this time, houses, and brethren, and sisters, and mothers, and children, and lands, with persecutions; and in the world to come eternal life".*** *Mark 10:28-30.*

When confronted with the question of the greatest commandment that must be observed to inherit everlasting life, and the clarity regarding one's neighbor, Jesus gave a profound parable. In the parable, Jesus illustrated clearly what God regards as love for one's neighbor. ***"And, behold, a certain lawyer stood up, and tempted him, saying, Master, what shall I do to inherit eternal life? [26] He said unto him, What is written in the law? how readest thou? [27] And he answering said, Thou shalt love the Lord thy God with all thy heart, and with all thy soul, and with all thy strength, and with all thy mind; and thy neighbour as thyself. [28] And he said unto him, Thou hast answered right: this do, and thou shalt live. [29] But he, willing to justify himself, said unto Jesus, And who is my neighbour? [30] And Jesus answering said, A certain man went down from Jerusalem to Jericho, and fell among thieves, which stripped***

him of his raiment, and wounded him, and departed, leaving him half dead. [31] And by chance there came down a certain priest that way: and when he saw him, he passed by on the other side. [32] And likewise a Levite, when he was at the place, came and looked on him, and passed by on the other side. [33] But a certain Samaritan, as he journeyed, came where he was: and when he saw him, he had compassion on him, [34] And went to him, and bound up his wounds, pouring in oil and wine, and set him on his own beast, and brought him to an inn, and took care of him. [35] And on the morrow when he departed, he took out two pence, and gave them to the host, and said unto him, Take care of him; and whatsoever thou spendest more, when I come again, I will repay thee. [36] Which now of these three, thinkest thou, was neighbour

unto him that fell among the thieves? [37] And he said, He that shewed mercy on him. Then said Jesus unto him, Go, and do thou likewise". *Luke 10:25-37.*

Jesus addressed the issue of duty to the state and authorities when he was confronted by the Pharisees regarding the payment of taxes to the government. ***"And they send unto him certain of the Pharisees and of the Herodians, to catch him in his words. [14] And when they were come, they say unto him, Master, we know that thou art true, and carest for no man: for thou regardest not the person of men, but teachest the way of God in truth: Is it lawful to give tribute to Caesar, or not? [15] Shall we give, or shall we not give? But he, knowing their hypocrisy, said unto them, Why tempt ye me? Bring me a penny, that I may see it. [16] And they brought it. And he***

saith unto them, Whose is this image and superscription? And they said unto him, Caesar's. [17] And Jesus answering said unto them, Render to Caesar the things that are Caesar's, and to God the things that are God's. And they marvelled at him". *Mark 12:13-17.*

Jesus corrected Peter when he answered the tribute collectors that Jesus does not pay tribute. He rather instructed Peter to pay the tribute for both of them in keeping with the requirements of the law and their obligation to the authorities. ***"And when they were come to Capernaum, they that received tribute money came to Peter, and said, Doth not your master pay tribute? [25] He saith, Yes. And when he was come into the house, Jesus prevented him, saying, What thinkest thou, Simon? of whom do the kings of the earth take custom or tribute? of***

their own children, or of strangers? [26] Peter saith unto him, Of strangers. Jesus saith unto him, Then are the children free. [27] Notwithstanding, lest we should offend them, go thou to the sea, and cast an hook, and take up the fish that first cometh up; and when thou hast opened his mouth, thou shalt find a piece of money: that take, and give unto them for me and thee". *Matthew 17:24-27.*

18

BOLD AND DARING

Jesus manifested the Spirit of Might during his ministry on Earth. The Lord was very bold and daring in his proclamations and in his preaching. Each time he spoke, the people were amazed at his words and wondered where he got his audacity from. They usually observed that he talked like someone with authority. In one of his encounters with the Jews at the Temple in Jerusalem, he claimed equality with God and earned the wrath of the Jews. ***"Then came the Jews round about him, and said unto him, How long dost thou make us to doubt? If thou be the Christ, tell us plainly. [25] Jesus answered them,***

I told you, and ye believed not: the works that I do in my Father's name, they bear witness of me. [26] But ye believe not, because ye are not of my sheep, as I said unto you. [27] My sheep hear my voice, and I know them, and they follow me: [28] And I give unto them eternal life; and they shall never perish, neither shall any man pluck them out of my hand. [29] My Father, which gave them me, is greater than all; and no man is able to pluck them out of my Father's hand. [30] I and my Father are one. [31] Then the Jews took up stones again to stone him. [32] Jesus answered them, Many good works have I shewed you from my Father; for which of those works do ye stone me? [33] The Jews answered him, saying, For a good work we stone thee not; but for blasphemy; and because that thou, being a man, makest thyself God". *John 10:24-33.*

His response was considered a blasphemy because he claimed equality with God, therefore making himself a Son of God. Jesus was well aware of the risk associated with such claims especially among the Jews, but he was not deterred. At the Synagogue in Nazareth where he was brought up, he told the people in the Synagogue that he is the fulfillment of the scripture, ***"And he came to Nazareth, where he had been brought up: and, as his custom was, he went into the synagogue on the Sabbath day, and stood up for to read. [17] And there was delivered unto him the book of the prophet Esaias. And when he had opened the book, he found the place where it was written, [18] The Spirit of the Lord is upon me, because he hath anointed me to preach the gospel to the poor; he hath sent me to heal the brokenhearted, to***

preach deliverance to the captives, and recovering of sight to the blind, to set at liberty them that are bruised, [19] To preach the acceptable year of the Lord. [20] And he closed the book, and he gave it again to the minister, and sat down. And the eyes of all them that were in the synagogue were fastened on him. [21] And he began to say unto them, This day is this scripture fulfilled in your ears". *Luke 4:16-21.*

During his conversation with his disciples, when asked by Philip to show them the Father, Jesus told them that, 'to have seen him is to have seen the Father'. By this, he was bold to say that he is the express image of God. ***"If ye had known me, ye should have known my Father also: and from henceforth ye know him, and have seen him. [8] Philip saith unto him, Lord, shew us the Father, and it sufficeth us. [9] Jesus***

saith unto him, Have I been so long time with you, and yet hast thou not known me, Philip? He that hath seen me hath seen the Father; and how sayest thou then, Shew us the Father? [10] Believest thou not that I am in the Father, and the Father in me? The words that I speak unto you I speak not of myself: but the Father that dwelleth in me, he doeth the works. [11] Believe me that I am in the Father, and the Father in me: or else believe me for the very works' sake". *John 14:7-11.*

The Lord Jesus was very daring to expressly say that he is the way, the truth and the life. By this assertion, he claimed to be the only access to God available to any man. ***"Thomas saith unto him, Lord, we know not whither thou goest; and how can we know the way? [6] Jesus saith unto him, I am the way, the truth, and the***

life: no man cometh unto the Father, but by me". *John 14:5-6.*

In one of the most dramatic and yet very significant incident during his ministry on Earth, the lord made one of the most profound statements ever made by any one. When accosted my Martha for failing to come speedily and heal her brother before his death, Jesus said he is the resurrection and the life. And he actually went ahead to prove it by raising Lazarus from the dead. ***"Now a certain man was sick, named Lazarus, of Bethany, the town of Mary and her sister Martha. [2] (It was that Mary which anointed the Lord with ointment, and wiped his feet with her hair, whose brother Lazarus was sick.) [3] Therefore his sisters sent unto him, saying, Lord, behold, he whom thou lovest is sick. [4] When Jesus heard that, he said, This*** *sickness is not unto death, but for the glory of God, that the Son of God might be glorified thereby. [5] Now Jesus loved Martha, and her sister, and Lazarus. [6] When he had heard therefore that he was sick, he abode two days still in the same place where he was. [7] Then after that saith he to his disciples, Let us go into Judaea again. [8] His disciples say unto him, Master, the Jews of late sought to stone thee; and goest thou thither again? [9] Jesus answered, Are there not twelve hours in the day? If any man walk in the day, he stumbleth not, because he seeth the light of this world. [10] But if a man walk in the night, he stumbleth, because there is no light in him. [11] These things said he: and after that he saith unto them, Our friend Lazarus sleepeth; but I go, that I may awake him out of sleep. [12] Then said his*

disciples, Lord, if he sleep, he shall do well. [13] Howbeit Jesus spake of his death: but they thought that he had spoken of taking of rest in sleep. [14] Then said Jesus unto them plainly, Lazarus is dead. [15] And I am glad for your sakes that I was not there, to the intent ye may believe; nevertheless let us go unto him. [16] Then said Thomas, which is called Didymus, unto his fellow disciples, Let us also go, that we may die with him. [17] Then when Jesus came, he found that he had lain in the grave four days already. [18] Now Bethany was nigh unto Jerusalem, about fifteen furlongs off: [19] And many of the Jews came to Martha and Mary, to comfort them concerning their brother. [20] Then Martha, as soon as she heard that Jesus was coming, went and met him: but Mary sat still in the house. [21] Then said Martha unto

Jesus, Lord, if thou hadst been here, my brother had not died. [22] But I know, that even now, whatsoever thou wilt ask of God, God will give it thee. [23] Jesus saith unto her, Thy brother shall rise again. [24] Martha saith unto him, I know that he shall rise again in the resurrection at the last day. [25] Jesus said unto her, I am the resurrection, and the life: he that believeth in me, though he were dead, yet shall he live: [26] And whosoever liveth and believeth in me shall never die. Believest thou this? [27] She saith unto him, Yea, Lord: I believe that thou art the Christ, the Son of God, which should come into the world". *John 11:1-27.*

Here Jesus taught that anyone who believes in him will never die. What a Lord! His gift of eternal life guarantees life both here and in the world to come. Praise God! The Lord expects each one of us to boldly declare him before men. The profession of our faith in the Lord Jesus must not be done in secret but openly before men. The Lord expressly declared, ***"Whosoever therefore shall confess me before men, him will I confess also before my Father which is in heaven. [33] But whosoever shall deny me before men, him will I also deny before my Father which is in heaven".*** *Matthew 10:32-33.*

Failure to openly and publicly declare his Lordship over our lives will expose us to outright denial of us before his Father and the angels of God in heaven on the last day. ***"Also I say unto you, Whosoever shall confess me before men, him shall the Son of man also confess before the angels of God: [9] But he that denieth me before men shall be denied before the angels of God".*** *Luke 12:8-9.*

In one of his conversations with the Jews, Jesus not only said he was before Abraham but referred to himself as 'I Am'. This was considered blasphemous because the Jews recognized God as the only one who has ever referred to himself as 'I AM' when he spoke to Moses in the Wilderness. This ambitious claim provoked them to pick up stones to kill him. ***"Your father Abraham rejoiced to see my day: and he saw it, and was glad. [57] Then said the Jews unto him, Thou art not yet fifty years old, and hast thou seen Abraham? [58] Jesus said unto them, Verily, verily, I say unto you, Before Abraham was, I am. [59] Then took they up stones to cast at him: but Jesus hid himself, and went out of the temple, going through the midst of them, and so passed by".***

John 8:56-59.

The Lord was bold enough to testify of his deity even in the face of public humiliation and execution. During his teaching ministry, the lord taught his followers to be very careful with the behaviors and acts of the Scribes and the Pharisees. He openly criticized their work and hypocrisy. However, he encouraged the people to obey the laws taught by them since they sit on Moses' seat. Most Jews would not dare challenge or criticize these people in authority for fear of being excommunicated from the temple and the Synagogues. Jesus challenged them to change their ways and live according to the precepts of the law. ***"Then spake Jesus to the multitude, and to his disciples, [2] Saying, The scribes and the Pharisees sit in Moses' seat: [3] All therefore whatsoever they bid you observe, that observe and do; but do not ye after their works: for they***

say, and do not. [4] For they bind heavy burdens and grievous to be borne, and lay them on men's shoulders; but they themselves will not move them with one of their fingers. [5] But all their works they do for to be seen of men: they make broad their phylacteries, and enlarge the borders of their garments, [6] And love the uppermost rooms at feasts, and the chief seats in the synagogues, [7] And greetings in the markets, and to be called of men, Rabbi, Rabbi. [8] But be not ye called Rabbi: for one is your Master, even Christ; and all ye are brethren. [9] And call no man your father upon the earth: for one is your Father, which is in heaven. [10] Neither be ye called masters: for one is your Master, even Christ. [13] But woe unto you, scribes and Pharisees, hypocrites! For ye shut up the kingdom of heaven against men: for ye

neither go in yourselves, neither suffer ye them that are entering to go in. [14] Woe unto you, scribes and Pharisees, hypocrites! For ye devour widows' houses, and for a pretence make long prayer: therefore ye shall receive the greater damnation. [15] Woe unto you, scribes and Pharisees, hypocrites! For ye compass sea and land to make one proselyte, and when he is made, ye make him twofold more the child of hell than yourselves. [16] Woe unto you, ye blind guides, which say, Whosoever shall swear by the temple, it is nothing; but whosoever shall swear by the gold of the temple, he is a debtor! [17] Ye fools and blind: for whether is greater, the gold, or the temple that sanctifieth the gold? [18] And, Whosoever shall swear by the altar, it is nothing; but whosoever sweareth by the gift that is upon it, he is guilty. [19] Ye fools and blind: for

whether is greater, the gift, or the altar that sanctifieth the gift? [20] Whoso therefore shall swear by the altar, sweareth by it, and by all things thereon. [21] And whoso shall swear by the temple, sweareth by it, and by him that dwelleth therein. [22] And he that shall swear by heaven, sweareth by the throne of God, and by him that sitteth thereon. [23] Woe unto you, scribes and Pharisees, hypocrites! For ye pay tithe of mint and anise and cummin, and have omitted the weightier matters of the law, judgment, mercy, and faith: these ought ye to have done, and not to leave the other undone. [24] Ye blind guides, which strain at a gnat, and swallow a camel. [25] Woe unto you, scribes and Pharisees, hypocrites! For ye make clean the outside of the cup and of the platter but within they are full of extortion and excess. [26] Thou

blind Pharisee, cleanse first that which is within the cup and platter that the outside of them may be clean also. [27] Woe unto you, scribes and Pharisees, hypocrites! for ye are like unto whited sepulchres, which indeed appear beautiful outward, but are within full of dead men's bones, and of all uncleanness. [28] Even so ye also outwardly appear righteous unto men, but within ye are full of hypocrisy and iniquity. [29] Woe unto you, scribes and Pharisees, hypocrites! Because ye build the tombs of the prophets, and garnish the sepulchres of the righteous". *Matthew 23:1-10, :13-29.*

For the very first time in human history, someone showed that he had the power and authority to forgive sin against God. The bible recorded an incident in the gospel of Matthew, where Jesus openly forgave a man sick of palsy his sins and ministered healing to him. This was to the amazement of the people standing by. "***And again he entered into Capernaum after some days; and it was noised that he was in the house. [2] And straightway many were gathered together, insomuch that there was no room to receive them, no, not so much as about the door: and he preached the word unto them. [3] And they come unto him, bringing one sick of the palsy, which was borne of four. [4] And when they could not come nigh unto him for the press, they uncovered the roof where he was: and when they had broken it up, they let down the bed wherein the sick of the palsy lay. [5] When Jesus saw their faith, he said unto the sick of the palsy, Son, thy sins be forgiven thee. [6] But there were certain of the scribes sitting there, and reasoning in their hearts, [7] Why doth this***

man thus speak blasphemies? Who can forgive sins but God only? [8] And immediately when Jesus perceived in his spirit that they so reasoned within themselves, he said unto them, Why reason ye these things in your hearts? [9] Whether is it easier to say to the sick of the palsy, Thy sins be forgiven thee; or to say, Arise, and take up thy bed, and walk? [10] But that ye may know that the Son of man hath power on earth to forgive sins, (he saith to the sick of the palsy,) [11] I say unto thee, Arise, and take up thy bed, and go thy way into thine house. [12] And immediately he arose, took up the bed, and went forth before them all; insomuch that they were all amazed and glorified God, saying, We never saw it on this fashion". *Mark 2:1-12.*

Jesus made a very strong assertion about himself when he said, he is the light. Light is that which defines, and reveals. By calling himself light, he insists that he is the model for life, uprightness and godliness. He went further to say that he is the light of the world and invites people to follow him and not walk in darkness, but enjoy the light of life. ***"As long as I am in the world, I am the light of the world".*** John 9:5. And "***Then spake Jesus again unto them, saying, I am the light of the world: he that followeth me shall not walk in darkness, but shall have the light of life".*** *John 8:12.*

He also said ***"I am come a light into the world, that whosoever believeth on me should not abide in darkness".*** *John 12:46.*

Apostle John in his gospel made a significant statement about Christ as the light of the world. ***"That was the true Light, which***

lighteth every man that cometh into the world" *John 1:9.*

As the light of God given to men, Jesus came to liberate men from the domain of darkness and to translate them into God's kingdom of light. This light has the power to expel the dominion and works of darkness. Jesus went further to call his followers lights. Matthew in his gospel recorded a statement made by Jesus referring to his followers as lights in the world, ***"Ye are the light of the world. A city that is set on an hill cannot be hid. [15] Neither do men light a candle, and put it under a bushel, but on a candlestick; and it giveth light unto all that are in the house. [16] Let your light so shine before men, that they may see your good works, and glorify your Father which is in heaven".*** *Matthew 5:14-16.*

He indicated that those who receive him automatically become sons of light and lights to their world. Apostle Paul referred to this new status of children of God when he said, ***"Do all things without murmurings and disputings: [15] That ye may be blameless and harmless, the sons of God, without rebuke, in the midst of a crooked and perverse nation, among whom ye shine as lights in the world".***
Philippians 2:14-15.

To demonstrate his power over the elements of nature, Jesus rebuked the wind and the storm while in a boat with his disciples. With a word of his mouth, the Master rebuked the stormy sea causing peace and calm to be restored. As lord of all creation, Jesus spoke peace to the troubled waters to the amazement of his disciples in the boat. ***"And the same day, when the even was***

come, he saith unto them, Let us pass over unto the other side. [36] And when they had sent away the multitude, they took him even as he was in the ship. And there were also with him other little ships. [37] And there arose a great storm of wind, and the waves beat into the ship, so that it was now full. [38] And he was in the hinder part of the ship, asleep on a pillow: and they awake him, and say unto him, Master, carest thou not that we perish? [39] And he arose, and rebuked the wind, and said unto the sea, Peace, be still. And the wind ceased, and there was a great calm. [40] And he said unto them, Why are ye so fearful? How is it that ye have no faith? [41] And they feared exceedingly, and said one to another, What manner of man is this, that even the wind and the sea obey him?"

Mark 4:35-41.

During his trial, when Jesus was being examined by the Roman governor, Pontius Pilate, Jesus ignored the governor's questions. Pilate was shocked and wondered why Jesus was unwilling to defend himself in the face of malignant accusations. When he answered Pilate, Jesus boldly told him clearly that he [Pilate] has no power over him. ***"And went again into the judgment hall, and saith unto Jesus, Whence art thou? But Jesus gave him no answer. [10] Then saith Pilate unto him, Speakest thou not unto me? knowest thou not that I have power to crucify thee, and have power to release thee? [11] Jesus answered, Thou couldest have no power at all against me, except it were given thee from above: therefore he that delivered me unto thee hath the greater sin".***

John 19:9-11.

While hanging on the cross in the middle of two criminals, Jesus unperturbed by his present condition was bold enough to assure the repentant thief a place in paradise. ***"And one of the malefactors which were hanged railed on him, saying, If thou be Christ, save thyself and us. [40] But the other answering rebuked him, saying, Dost not thou fear God, seeing thou art in the same condemnation? [41] And we indeed justly; for we receive the due reward of our deeds: but this man hath done nothing amiss. [42] And he said unto Jesus, Lord, remember me when thou comest into thy kingdom. [43] And Jesus said unto him, Verily I say unto thee, Today shalt thou be with me in paradise".***
Luke 23:39-43.

On one occasion after his resurrection, Jesus met his disciples and told them that all power in heaven and on earth has been given to him. That is a huge and very deep statement. ***"Then the eleven disciples went away into Galilee, into a mountain where Jesus had appointed them. [17] And when they saw him, they worshipped him: but some doubted. [18] And Jesus came and spake unto them, saying, All power is given unto me in heaven and in earth".*** *Matthew 28:16-18*

This means that he not only has absolute powers on earth but enjoys same in heaven. His power is totally absolute. That is awesome! Jesus is the head of the church and we are his body. His power is available to us as members of his body.

19

PATIENCE

The Lord Jesus while on Earth exhibited the highest level of patience with everyone in all his dealings. The decision to take the form of a man to serve as a sacrificial lamb was most uncommon. Referring to this uncommon choice, Apostle Paul wrote, ***"Let this mind be in you, which was also in Christ Jesus: [6] Who, being in the form of God, thought it not robbery to be equal with God: [7] But made himself of no reputation, and took upon him the form of a servant, and was made in the likeness of men: [8] And being found in fashion as a man, he humbled himself, and became obedient unto***

death, even the death of the cross. [9] Wherefore God also hath highly exalted him, and given him a name which is above every name: [10] That at the name of Jesus every knee should bow, of things in heaven, and things in earth, and things under the earth; [11] And that every tongue should confess that Jesus Christ is Lord, to the glory of God the Father". *Philippians 2:5-11.*

Specifically talking about his deep sense of patience, the bible recorded; ***"Looking unto Jesus the author and finisher of our faith; who for the joy that was set before him endured the cross, despising the shame, and is set down at the right hand of the throne of God, [3] For consider him that endured such contradiction of sinners against himself, lest ye be wearied and faint in your minds".***

Hebrews 12:2-3.

One of the greatest virtues required as children of God is patience. Patience is the ability to bear pains or trials without complaining. A patient person is steadfast despite difficulty, opposition or adversity. The Lord Jesus demonstrated this quality and capacity while on earth especially during his passion and crucifixion on the cross. In the book of Hebrews the bible recorded concerning Jesus, ***"Though he were a Son, yet learned he obedience by the things which he suffered; [9] And being made perfect, he became the author of eternal salvation unto all them that obey him"***
Hebrews 5:8-9.

This posture was also expressed in the second chapter of the same book, ***"Thou hast put all things in subjection under his feet. For in that he put all in subjection under him, he left***

nothing that is not put under him. But now we see not yet all things put under him. [9] But we see Jesus, who was made a little lower than the angels for the suffering of death, crowned with glory and honour; that he by the grace of God should taste death for every man. [10] For it became him, for whom are all things, and by whom are all things, in bringing many sons unto glory, to make the captain of their salvation perfect through sufferings". *Hebrews 2:8-10.*

In his letter to the Corinthians church, Apostle Paul taught that God has given us the grace and ability to forebear any challenge. ***"There hath no temptation taken you but such as is common to man: but God is faithful, who will not suffer you to be tempted above that ye are able; but will with the temptation also make***

a way to escape, that ye may be able to bear it". *1 Corinthians 10:13.*

Jesus taught his disciples that patience is an important ingredient for effectual spiritual productivity. Talking about the productivity of the various hearts in his parable of the sower, the Lord said, ***"But that on the good ground are they, which in an honest and good heart, having heard the word, keep it, and bring forth fruit with patience".*** *Luke 8:15.*

Apostle James made a remarkable statement in his epistle regarding the role of patience in the growth and maturity of a Christian. Although faith grows with the increase of God's word we receive, until our faith is tested, proven or tried, it cannot be strengthened. Strong faith comes with the trials and tribulations which serve to prove our faith. Therefore even a big or large faith could be weak when it is unable [or fails] to withstand the storms of adversity and temptations. ***"My brethren, count it all joy when ye fall into divers temptations; [3] Knowing this, that the trying of your faith worketh patience. [4] But let patience have her perfect work, that ye may be perfect and entire, wanting nothing".*** *James 1:2-4.*

The ability to overcome temptations, trials and tribulations makes the child of God perfect or mature and thus able to assume higher responsibilities in the kingdom of God. Apostle Paul in his letter to the church in Rome explained this principle further when he said, ***"Therefore being justified by faith, we have peace with God through our Lord Jesus Christ: [2] By whom also we have access by faith into this grace wherein we stand, and rejoice in hope of the***

glory of God. [3] And not only so, but we glory in tribulations also: knowing that tribulation worketh patience; [4] And patience, experience; and experience, hope: [5] And hope maketh not ashamed; because the love of God is shed abroad in our hearts by the Holy Ghost which is given unto us". *Romans 5:1-5.*

The bible also talks about the reward that comes with patience when faith is tried in the life of a believer. ***"That ye be not slothful, but followers of them who through faith and patience inherit the promises. [13] For when God made promise to Abraham, because he could swear by no greater, he sware by himself, [14] Saying, Surely blessing I will bless thee, and multiplying I will multiply thee. [15] And so, after he had patiently endured, he obtained the promise".*** *Hebrews 6:12-15.*

Furthermore the bible says, ***"Cast not away therefore your confidence, which hath great recompense of reward. [36] For ye have need of patience, that, after ye have done the will of God, ye might receive the promise".*** *Hebrews 10:35-36.*

We are therefore encouraged to run our race with patience as our Lord did and got his reward. ***"Wherefore seeing we also are compassed about with so great a cloud of witnesses, let us lay aside every weight, and the sin which doth so easily beset us, and let us run with patience the race that is set before us, [2] Looking unto Jesus the author and finisher of our faith; who for the joy that was set before him endured the cross, despising the shame, and is set down at the right hand of the throne of God. [3] For consider him that endured such***

contradiction of sinners against himself, lest ye be wearied and faint in your minds".
Hebrews 12:1-3.

Patience is a clear mark of Christian maturity. This was outlined by Apostle Paul in his letter to Titus, ***"But speak thou the things which become sound doctrine: [2] That the aged men be sober, grave, temperate, sound in faith, in charity, in patience".*** *Titus 2:1-2.*

Apostle Peter went further to explain that our effectiveness and fulfillment as Christians requires patience, ***"Grace and peace be multiplied unto you through the knowledge of God, and of Jesus our Lord, [3] According as his divine power hath given unto us all things that pertain unto life and godliness, through the knowledge of him that hath called us to glory and virtue: [4] Whereby are given unto us***

exceeding great and precious promises: that by these ye might be partakers of the divine nature, having escaped the corruption that is in the world through lust. [5] And beside this, giving all diligence, add to your faith virtue; and to virtue knowledge; [6] And to knowledge temperance; and to temperance patience; and to patience godliness; [7] And to godliness brotherly kindness; and to brotherly kindness charity. [8] For if these things be in you, and abound, they make you that ye shall neither be barren nor unfruitful in the knowledge of our Lord Jesus Christ. [9] But he that lacketh these things is blind, and cannot see afar off, and hath forgotten that he was purged from his old sins. [10] Wherefore the rather, brethren, give diligence to make your calling and election

sure: for if ye do these things, ye shall never fall". *2 Peter 1:2-10.*

In his letter to Timothy, Apostle Paul instructs believers to guard against covetousness and the deceitfulness of riches by walking in patience and other godly virtues. ***"Perverse disputing of men of corrupt minds, and destitute of the truth, supposing that gain is godliness: from such withdraw thyself. [6] But godliness with contentment is great gain. [7] For we brought nothing into this world, and it is certain we can carry nothing out. [8] And having food and raiment let us be therewith content. [9] But they that will be rich fall into temptation and a snare, and into many foolish and hurtful lusts, which drown men in destruction and perdition. [10] For the love of money is the root of all evil: which while some coveted after, they have erred***

from the faith, and pierced themselves through with many sorrows. [11] But thou, O man of God, flee these things; and follow after righteousness, godliness, faith, love, patience, meekness. [12] Fight the good fight of faith, lay hold on eternal life, whereunto thou art also called, and hast professed a good profession before many witnesses". *1Timothy 6:5-12.*

If you do not have a relationship with Jesus, I invite you to make the most important decision and have the most vital relationship in life. Please say this prayer aloud and mean it with all your heart:

O LORD God, I believe in my heart that Jesus is the Son of God. I believe that he died for me and God raised him from the dead. I confess with my mouth that Jesus is the Lord of my life. Please wash me with the precious blood of Jesus. I receive eternal life into my spirit. I am born again. I am now a child of God. Thank you for saving me. In the name of the Lord Jesus, amen.